Legal Culture and Identity in Central and Eastern Europe

Central and Eastern European Forum for Legal, Political, and Social Theory Yearbook

Edited by Jürgen Busch, Péter Cserne, Michael Hein, Miklós Könczöl, Miodrag Jovanović, and Marta Soniewicka

Volume 13

Áron Fábián and Márton Matyasovszky-Németh (eds.)

Legal Culture and Identity in Central and Eastern Europe

PETER LANG
Berlin · Bruxelles · Chennai · Lausanne · New York · Oxford

Bibliographic Information published by the Deutsche Nationalbibliothek
The Deutsche Nationalbibliothek lists this publication in the Deutsche Nationalbibliografie; detailed bibliographic data is available online at http://dnb.d-nb.de.

Library of Congress Cataloging-in-Publication Data
Names: Fábián, Áron, 1994- editor | Matyasovszky-Németh, Márton, 1993- editor
Title: Legal culture and identity in Central and Eastern Europe / Áron Fábián, Márton Matyasovszky-Németh (eds.).
Description: Berlin; New York: Peter Lang, 2026. | Series: Central and Eastern European Forum for Legal, Political, and Social Theory yearbook, 2191-8317; volume 13 | Includes bibliographical references and index.
Identifiers: LCCN 2026011312 (print) | LCCN 2026011313 (ebook) | ISBN 9783631908556 hardback | ISBN 9783631941379 pdf | ISBN 9783631944035 epub
Subjects: LCSH: Culture and law--Europe, Central | Culture and law--Europe, Eastern | Constitutional law--Europe, Central | Constitutional law--Europe, Eastern | Socialism--Europe, Central--History | Socialism--Europe, Eastern--History | Identity politics--Europe, Central | Identity politics--Europe, Eastern | European Union countries--Economic integration
Classification: LCC KJC6257.L43 2026 (print) | LCC KJC6257 (ebook)
LC record available at https://lccn.loc.gov/2026011312
LC ebook record available at https://lccn.loc.gov/2026011313

Publication of the volume was made possible by the kind financial support of Eötvös Loránd University, Budapest, Hungary.

ISSN 2191-8317
ISBN 978-3-631-90855-6 (Print)
ISBN 978-3-631-94137-9 (ePDF)
ISBN 978-3-631-94403-5 (ePUB)
DOI 10.3726/b23244

Published by Peter Lang GmbH, Berlin (Germany)

info@peterlang.com

This publication has been peer reviewed.

www.peterlang.com

Contact for General Product Safety Regulation (GPSR): gpsr@peterlang.com

Contents

Introduction

Áron Fábián and Márton Matyasovszky-Németh

We are very happy to present the next volume of the long-running Central and Eastern European Forum for Legal, Political, and Social Theory Yearbook series. This collection of chapters, presented at the 14th Central and Eastern European Forum of Young Legal, Political, and Social Theorists held in Budapest, Hungary, between October 6 and 7, 2022, at the Bibó István College for Advanced Studies, Eötvös Loránd University, explores the theme of "Legal Culture and Identity in Central and Eastern Europe."

Legal culture has become a focal point for socio-legal scholars, generating lively discourse through both theoretical attempts to conceptualize and categorize legal cultures and empirical research efforts to measure them. This heightened interest has brought with it a multiplicity of debates warranting further discussion, especially in Central and Eastern Europe. The region's historical, geological, sociological, and political ties make it an excellent case study of legal cultures. The countries in the region share deep historical ties, both through the empires of old with their Austrian and German influence on the legal systems, as well as the shared experience of a socialist past. Since the regime changes of 1989, the countries in the region have all been influenced by the emerging body of EU law and the vision of a *Ius Commune Europaeum*.

The experience of life on the periphery, both a curse and a blessing, has given rise to influential theoretical contributions such as Eugen Ehrlich's living law, fueled by the reception of imperial law. This experience of periphery is key to understanding and conceptualizing a Central European Legal Family. At the same time, we are seeing a resurgence of national legal and constitutional identities, increasingly used as argumentative tools for emphasizing national characteristics and interests in the face of ever-closer integration. Scholarly discourse from multiple countries in the region might illuminate what we mean by constitutional identity, what the constitutional identities of different countries entail, and how they might influence each other.

For this volume, the editors invited scholars to think about what binds Central and Eastern European legal systems together and what divides them. How does the experience of periphery influence our legal systems and legal theory? How should we characterize our legal cultures? What implications does this have on comparative analysis? What do we make of the increasingly popular notion of national constitutional identity?

We welcomed contributions that engage these topics from a complex socio-legal perspective, including theories of legal culture in Central and Eastern Europe, characteristics of Central and Eastern European legal cultures, experiences of periphery and its impact on social theory, the Central and Eastern Legal Family: myth or reality, experiences of Empire and Socialist law in Central and Eastern Europe, and Central and Eastern European constitutional identities.

This first chapter by Chris Hann explores the socioeconomic conditions and intellectual production of populist ideologies in Hungary from the 1930s to the 2020s. Hann begins by acknowledging his outsider perspective as an anthropologist and his focus on rural Hungary. He discusses the populist (*népi*) writers' movement of the 1930s, highlighting figures like Gyula Illyés and Ferenc Erdei, who documented rural poverty and socioeconomic backwardness. Hann examines the populist values of the pre-socialist era and their evolution during the socialist decades, noting the impact of socialist policies on rural communities. He concludes by discussing the post-socialist period, the rise of Viktor Orbán's Fidesz party, and the ongoing polarization in Hungarian society.

Hann delves into the inter-war period, generally considered the principal Hungarian flowering of a movement with analogies elsewhere in Eastern Europe dating back to the nineteenth century. He traces the origins of Hungarian populism to Romanticism and Herderian impulses of the counter-Enlightenment. The defeat of the 1848–9 revolution and the consolidation of the dual monarchy after 1867 left no political space for populist politics, dominated by Christian conservative nationalism. Hann highlights the Golden Age for *falukutatás* (village research) following the March Front of 1937, exemplified by the trilogy of books published under the title *Magyarország felfedezése* [The Discovery of Hungary]. Hann then explores the vicissitudes of the socialist era, characterized by failed revolution and repression. He argues that the symbiotic relationship between communism and populism led to the transcendence of the *népi-urbánus* opposition by new forms of citizenship. He highlights the revival of the monograph series *Magyarország felfedezése* in 1970 and the influence of populist imaginaries in urban spheres, such as the *táncház* movement.

Hann examines the tensions between town and countryside in the campaigning ahead of the democratic elections of 1990. He ends by discussing the rise of Viktor Orbán's Fidesz party and the ideological initiative seized by Orbán after his defeat in 2002. Hann theorizes the new populism in the context of accelerating globalization and neoliberal decades, arguing that *populista* currents become dangerous, undermining the rule of law both at home and in the EU context. He concludes by connecting the three phases of Hungarian populism: an emancipatory literary movement, a symbiotic relationship with socialist modernity, and an anti-pluralist reaction to neoliberal capitalist globalization.

Next, Balázs Fekete's contribution introduces Pierre Legrand's approach to comparative legal studies, which challenges the orthodox, positivist methodology. He argues that Central European legal studies often neglect the cultural and social contexts of legal phenomena. Fekete critiques two volumes, "Comparative Constitutionalism in Central Europe" and "European Legal Cultures in Transition," for their positivist approach and lack of contextual sensitivity. He advocates for a more nuanced understanding of legal transplants and the role of local culture in shaping legal norms.

Fekete advocates Legrand's radically different approach to comparative legal studies, highlighting the need to rethink and renew the toolkit of traditional comparative law. He emphasizes the importance of understanding legal phenomena through their cultural and political contexts, arguing that conventional positivist approaches are insufficient. As an illustration, he examines two specific volumes that demonstrate the narrow, decontextualized orientation of Central European legal studies. He critiques the methodological premises of these works, arguing that they fail to account for the cultural and political background of the legal phenomena studied. Fekete explores the issue of legal transplants in Central and Eastern Europe, arguing that the phenomenon of glocalization is crucial for understanding the regional failures and successes of legal transplantation. He emphasizes the importance of considering local external legal cultures and the impact of legal alienation on legal mobilization.

Chapter 3 by Peter Čuroš examines the constitutional identity of the Slovak Constitutional Court (SCC). He discusses the historical development of constitutional review in Czechoslovakia and Slovakia, highlighting the influence of the Austrian and German legal traditions. Čuroš analyzes the

SCC's role in shaping the Slovak legal system, focusing on significant cases such as the Special Court decision, the appointment of the prosecutor general, and the Mečiar amnesties case. He argues that the SCC has struggled to find its identity, often serving as a tool for judicial and political interests. He argues that the SCC resembles more the Schmittian version of the constitutional court, rather than the Kelsenian one, serving as a guardian of the legal form rather than the constitution. By examining the SCC's struggle to establish its identity, he highlights the impact of judicial collegiality and political pressures on its decisions. He analyzes several noteworthy cases, such as the existence of the Special Court, the appointment of the prosecutor general, and the Mečiar amnesties case, arguing that the SCC has often served as a tool for furthering judicial and political interests. He concludes that the SCC's decisions reflect a tension between formalism and the need for a more substantive approach to constitutional review, often influenced by competing interests rather than a stable doctrine.

The next chapter by Adam Demczuk explores the concept of constitutional identity (CI) through the philosophical perspectives of David Hume and Thomas Hobbes, as well as psychological theories of group identity. He distinguishes between static and dynamic approaches to CI, arguing that dynamic models, such as those proposed by Gary J. Jacobsohn and Michel Rosenfeld, offer a more comprehensive understanding. Demczuk applies Hume's relational view of identity and Hobbes' distinctions between natural and artificial persons to the formation of CI. He also uses group identity theory to analyze the dimensions of importance, commitment, deference, and a sense of superiority within the constitutional subject.

Demczuk applies group identity theory to CI, focusing on the dimensions of importance, commitment, deference, and a sense of superiority. He argues that these dimensions help explain the perception of CI within the constitutional subject. For example, the importance dimension indicates the significance of a given role for the identity of the subject, while the commitment dimension involves changes in the perception of constitutional ideals. The deference dimension describes engagement in group norms and actions, and the sense of superiority entails the belief that one's group is better than others.

He concludes by advocating for a clear distinction between static and dynamic approaches to CI. He argues that static theories should be interpreted within a closed system of legal doctrine, while dynamic approaches should be studied in the fields of sociology, psychology, and political sciences. Demczuk emphasizes the importance of empirical qualitative research methods, such as thematic analysis, critical discourse analysis, and grounded theory, to further deepen the understanding of dynamic CI. He warns against the dangers of mixing static and dynamic theories and calls for a more nuanced and context-sensitive approach to studying CI.

Jozef Jenčík's contribution delves into the intricate dynamics of constitutional identities in Central and Eastern Europe, framed through the concept of the "Periphery Paradox." This paradox is rooted in Oswald Spengler's "The Decline of the West" and is analyzed using Hegelian paradoxes, particularly focusing on the idea that history is shaped by "slaves" rather than "masters," and that freedom arises from the toils of "slaves" rather than the rule of "masters."

Jenčík begins by discussing Spengler's ideas on the decline of Western civilization, emphasizing the intervention of abstract truths in the world of facts and the phenomenon of modern "Faustian" technology. The chapter then explores the core-periphery distinction, which is based on the distribution of power, resources, and knowledge. The core represents dominant regions, while the periphery comprises subordinate regions. This model extends beyond geography to influence politics, economics, and knowledge systems. Jenčík argues that the core-periphery dynamic is evident in the global economic system, international politics, and the dominance of Western theories and ideologies.

Jenčík highlights Hegel's influence on the concept of the periphery, particularly his assertion that history and freedom are shaped by the efforts of the oppressed rather than the rulers. This idea profoundly influenced Ľudovít Štúr and the Slovak national awakening. Štúr's political use of the periphery involved leveraging the structures of the periphery to resist assimilation into the Hungarian core, emphasizing the importance of the periphery in preserving national identity.

He then examines the contemporary political use of the periphery in Central and Eastern Europe. Jenčík discusses the emergence of constitutional identities in the region and the challenges posed by the dominance of Western liberal democracy. He argues that the periphery paradox is even more pronounced in the context of Western decline, with the periphery seeking distinctiveness while navigating the challenges of technocratic governance.

He argues that the most urgent challenge is to find effective mnemonic constitutionalism that goes beyond mere state reprisals and addresses the deeper cultural and political dynamics of the region.

Next, Piotr Zaleski's chapter addresses the issue of judicial activism in Poland through the lens of different traditional understandings of political power. He introduces Hannah Arendt's theoretical framework to highlight the distinction between the Hebrew-Christian, command-oriented tradition and the Greco-Roman, community-oriented tradition of political power. Zaleski argues that the contemporary Polish judiciary is caught between its republican heritage and liberal influences, reflecting a Janus-faced nature.

Zaleski argues that the contemporary Polish judiciary reflects a Janus-faced nature, caught between its republican heritage and liberal influences. He discusses the challenges posed by judicial activism, particularly in the context of the 2020 ruling on abortion, which sparked mass protests and highlighted the tension between judicial decisions and popular will.

He concludes by emphasizing the need for a balanced approach that respects the republican tradition of lawmaking while addressing the challenges posed by judicial activism. He argues that the Polish judiciary must navigate the tension between its historical roots and contemporary influences to effectively serve the needs of the society.

The editors hope that 14th CEE Forum of Young Legal, Political, and Social Theorists has brought together a diverse array of scholars to explore the intricate and multifaceted theme of "Legal Culture and Identity in Central and Eastern Europe." This volume, which compiles the chapters presented at the forum, offers a comprehensive examination of the region's legal cultures, constitutional identities, and the socio-political dynamics that shape them. Through the detailed analyses and critical perspectives provided by the contributors, several key themes and insights have emerged.

One of the central themes of this volume is the interplay between Legal Culture and Identity in Central and Eastern Europe. The region's unique historical, sociological, and political contexts have given rise to distinct legal cultures that are both influenced by and resistant to external forces. The contributions in this volume demonstrate the importance of both theoretical and empirical approaches to understanding such a unique and varied legal culture and identity. Theoretical frameworks, such as those provided by Pierre Legrand, David Hume, and Thomas Hobbes, offer valuable insights into the conceptualization of constitutional identity and the role of legal transplants. Empirical research, on the other hand, provides a grounded understanding of how these theoretical concepts play out in practice. The combination of these approaches allows for a more nuanced and comprehensive analysis of the region's legal phenomena.

The rise of populism in Central and Eastern Europe has also had a profound impact on legal culture and identity. The chapters on Hungary and Poland illustrate how populist ideologies have influenced legal and political developments in these countries. The exploration of the socioeconomic conditions that give rise to populism, the intellectual production of populist ideologies, and the impact of populist policies on legal institutions provide a comprehensive understanding of this phenomenon. The analysis of populism also highlights the broader implications for the rule of law, democratic governance, and constitutionalism in the region. The role of constitutional courts in shaping legal culture and identity is also a central focus. The chapters on the Slovak Constitutional Court and the Polish Constitutional Tribunal highlight the complex interplay between judicial activism, political interests, and the quest for constitutional identity.

As the Central and Eastern European regions continue to navigate the challenges of globalization, European integration, and internal political dynamics, the insights gained from this volume will be invaluable for scholars, policymakers, and practitioners alike. We hope that this collection will inspire further research and discussion on these important topics, fostering a deeper appreciation of the complexities and richness of Central and Eastern European legal cultures.

Socioeconomic Conditions and the Intellectual Production of "Populist" Ideologies: A Turbulent Century in Hungary, 1930s–2020s

Chris Hann

ABSTRACT

Chris Hann explores the links between socioeconomic conditions and production of populist ideologies in Hungary from the 1930s to the 2020s. His outsider perspective as a foreign anthropologist derives from his fieldwork in the countryside in the 1970s. He also outlines the contributions and compromises made over decades by several influential intellectuals, including Iván Boldizsár. The populist values of the pre-socialist era persisted and took new forms under socialism Hann notes the impact of socialist policies on rural communities, and concludes with a look at the political scene in Hungary today.

Keywords: Iván Boldizsár, populism in Hungary, urban-rural divide

Thank you for the invitation to speak to you today. I hesitated before accepting, for two reasons that I wish to emphasize from the start. First, I am not a Hungarian. My family has no links to East Central Europe. I lack the background, perhaps also some tacit knowledge, that those educated and using media in this country share. This is as important in this century in the era of social media as it was in the 1960s when Tamás Hofer distinguished between native ethnographers and comparative anthropologists based elsewhere. The "slash and burn" research of the latter could never match the depth of the former, who analyzed the culture in which they had been immersed all their lives.[1] Second, as an anthropologist I have focused on the countryside, and on people engaged in agricultural activities rather than administration or the production of knowledge. In practice, this meant that from the beginning of my field research in the village of Tázlár on the Danube-Tisza interfluve in the mid-1970s, I was interested in mundane, economic matters there. While other foreigners in Eastern Europe were enthralled by academic debates about how best to characterize "actually existing socialism," I largely ignored theory. This philistine approach would probably not have worked in any other discipline,

[1] Tamás Hofer, "Anthropologists and native ethnographers in Central European villages. Comparative notes on the professional personality of two disciplines" *Current Anthropology* 9 (1968) 311–15.

but it was acceptable in anthropology, at least in the Malinowskian school that emphasizes ethnography. Of course, I did read a bit about Hungarian history, and in particular the history of the relatively new community of Tázlár, a settlement which celebrates its 150th anniversary in 2022. I had numerous friends in Budapest who could have enlightened me about other kinds of history, outside the approved textbooks, including one who worked at the Lukács Archive. But since neither the history of political conflicts nor the history of ideas seemed to play a significant role for my interlocutors in Tázlár, most of whom were caught up in late socialist embourgeoisement processes,[2] these were not important subjects for me. It is now far too late for me to make good these deficits!

One partial exception to this extreme ignorance concerned the populist writers' movement of the 1930s, who were present in my consciousness for a number of reasons. One of the very few works by a contemporary Hungarian writer available in English was *People of the Puszta* by Gyula Illyés (1902–83), who I soon understood to be a literary giant. During my doctoral project, following the advice of Mihály Sárkány, a young researcher at the *Néprajzi Kutató Csoport* of the Academy of Sciences, I took particular interest in the early work of Ferenc Erdei, both his sociographic studies of the region in which Tázlár is located and his more analytic studies of "Hungarian peasant society" in interwar conditions that remained semi-feudal.[3] Illyés and Erdei were themselves born and brought up in the countryside. Later I worked for a year as an English language editor at the *New Hungarian Quarterly*, edited by Iván Boldizsár. I learned that you did not have to have a peasant background yourself in order to make valuable contributions to the populist documentation of rural conditions in the 1930s. In the 1930s, Boldizsár had edited two celebrated studies by his *Gimnázium* schoolmate Zoltán Szabó, *A Tardi helyzet* and *Cifra nyomorúság*. Their paths had diverged since 1949. Szabó did not return to Hungary after the trial of László Rajk, while Boldizsár became notorious for the compromises he made in order to remain a man of influence in Budapest, both in the dark years when the Communist Party was led by

2 Ivan Szelényi, *Socialist Entrepreneurs. Embourgeosisement in Rural Hungary* (University of Wisconsin Press 1986).

3 Ferenc Erdei, *Futóhomok*. A Duna-Tisza köze (Athenaeum 1937); *A magyar parasztttársadalom* (Franklin 1942).

Mátyás Rákosi and later throughout the long hegemony of János Kádár. But the two schoolmates maintained contact, perhaps even friendship; and so I learned that, to some degree at least, populist values could be embraced by Francophile intellectuals born and raised in the capital.

What were these values? How is one to define the Hungarian populism of that pre-socialist era in a new century in which the word has acquired strongly negative connotations in English? How can the same word be stretched to cover both *népi*, the Hungarian term for the writers and social scientists of the 1930s, and the *populista* currents associated with Viktor Orbán's Fidesz party, condemned as demagogic by liberals both at home and abroad? Is the polarization that many commentators have noted in today's Hungary really comparable to the opposition between *népi* and *urbánus* in the 1930s? I do not have answers to all these questions. But I would like you to keep them in mind during this lecture, and perhaps we can explore them further in the discussion. It would be absurd for a foreigner to waste your time with philological and semantic analysis of how words like *nép* and *nemzet* have evolved over centuries.[4] I take it for granted that to utter the word *populista* in Hungary today evokes entirely different resonances from the word *népi* in the 1930s, or indeed the 1980s and today. But rather than conclude erroneous translation or deplore the poverty of the English language, I hold on to the word populism in order to highlight the real subject of my talk, namely what I refer to in my title as changing socioeconomic conditions. There will be three sections, the longest of which will be about the populism of the later socialist decades.

1.1 Initial Flourishing, 1930s–1940s

First, let me say a little more about the interwar period, generally taken to be the principal Hungarian flowering of a movement that has many analogies elsewhere in Eastern Europe dating back deep into the nineteenth century. Origins can arguably be pushed back further still: to Romanticism, notably Herderian impulses of the counter-Enlightenment. The Russian case is the best known. Popularizing tendencies were strong in Hungarian literature.

[4] Gyula Borbándi, *Der ungarische Populismus* (Hase & Koehler 1976) offers a good introduction.

But after the defeat of the revolution of 1848–9 and consolidation of the dual monarchy after 1867, there was no political space for a populist politics. Politics was dominated by Christian conservative nationalism (even when the ruling party was nominally liberal). The urban economy was rapidly transformed, and German speakers and Jews were conspicuous in the wealthy elites. The disintegration of the empire after 1918 was followed by the regime of Miklós Horthy, authoritarian but allowing just enough freedom for the critical works I noted in my opening remarks. The years following the March Front of 1937 are the Golden Age for *falukutatás*, literally village research. A trilogy of books published in 1937–8 by Athenaeum under the title *Magyarország felfedezése* [The Discovery of Hungary] exemplified this work. Iván Boldizsár, for whom I worked as a language editor in 1979–80), was a key figure in this movement.

I already mentioned one of the books in this mini-series: *Futóhomok* [Running Sand] by Ferenc Erdei, which focused on the Danube-Tisza interfluve.[5] Erdei wrote movingly about rural poverty in locations such as Tázlár, dominated by isolated farms known as *tanyák* and lacking "any seed of a village" and modern civilization. Such places appeared at first glance to be the antithesis of the manorial communities described by Illyés in his sociographic memoir. Yet, as Erdei showed in a series of later publications, both were consequences of the country's socioeconomic backwardness in a rapidly modernizing Europe. The expanding capitalist economy was associated strongly with Jews and antisemitic tones can be detected in some analyses of the cleft between *népi* and *urbánus*. Many populists were Christian conservatives who drifted further to the right during the war. But Erdei's feelings for his country remained free of Fascist poisons. Committed to the left from his student days in Szeged, he was far from embracing Stalinist collectivization. As the animator of the onion cooperative in his native Makó,

5 Note 3. The others were Szabó's *Cifra nyomorúság* and *Viharsarok* by Géza Féja. Boldizsár was commissioned by the publisher to prepare a volume depicting social and political conditions in Hungary's far western counties, those which bordered on an Austria already incorporated into the Third Reich. He was familiar with the region from previous trips (initially as a Boy Scout). However, both copies of his draft manuscript were confiscated by the censor. As a result, *The Western Gate* (*A nyugati kapu*) was never published. Iván Boldizsár is remembered as an organizer and editor in the *falukutatás* movement, not as an author. See Iván Boldizsár, *Keser*-édes. (Magvető 1987) 85–6.

he visited western Europe and extolled how it was possible to modernize the countryside within a capitalist framework. Similar themes were addressed by Iván Boldizsár a few years later following a short visit to Denmark, which he celebrated as "the country of rich peasants."[6]

That the populists of this era had no common political platform became obvious during the Second World War and its aftermath. Some luminaries, notably Illyés himself, prioritized literature and were temperamentally unsuited to political agitation. Erdei was joined by numerous *népi* activists at the Szárszó Conference in 1943. But not all of those who had contributed critical works in the 1930s felt able to welcome Soviet forces and the prospect of a socialist regime. Zoltán Szabó did not go to Szárszó, thereby distancing himself from the *népi* core. But he and his new friend István Bibó[7] did join Erdei's National Peasant Party, which worked closely with Soviet forces from 1944 onward. Its electoral support was small in comparison with that obtained by the Independent Smallholders' Party, which emphasized Christian nationalism and was stridently anti-communist. This was the rural political constellation when party pluralism was eliminated, and the prominent populists went their separate ways. Some chose foreign emigration (notably Szabó, who worked for several decades as Radio Free Europe's London correspondent). Some, notably Bibó, remained in Hungary but were coerced into withdrawal from the public sphere (apart from the 1956 revolution, when he was a Minister). Some, notably Ferenc Erdei, occupied high office in the state and later in the Academy of Sciences.

1.2 Socialism, 1960s–1980s

I have no time to explore the vicissitudes of the 1950s, characterized by failed revolution and repression. The constituencies of the populists in the countryside were the principal casualties of these years. Peasants were subject to often arbitrary appropriations. Eventually, by 1961 the great majority of rural proprietors had been coerced into joining collective farms. They must have feared the worst. But the Hungarian *termelőszövetkezet* turned out to

6 Iván Boldizsár, *A gazdag parasztok országa* (Franklin 1940).

7 See Gábor Noszkai, "Bibó István és Szabó Zoltán barátságának története" (Parts 1 and 2) (2009–10) 14/11–15/1 *Beszélő*.

be a very different institution from the Soviet *kolkhoz*. From the early 1960s, and especially after the economic reforms introduced in 1968, farms became dynamic commercial actors in the socialist commodity economy. Thanks to the myriad forms of *háztáji*, material incentives penetrated the rural household. I argued in my doctoral research that the *szakszövetkezet* in Tázlár, which did not impose the usual consolidation of fields on its membership, was an extreme example of flexible processes that were key to Hungary's relative economic successes in those years.[8]

Until his death in 1971, Ferenc Erdei appears to have been an eminence grise encouraging these processes. But he was not alone. Countless officials of the Communist Party (including János Kádár himself) inculcated in the ideology of a militant workers' movement began, in the wake of 1956, to implement quite different approaches. It was critical for social peace and the furtherance of socialist goals in the long term that villagers be able to pursue their own forms of embourgeoisement. The old term *polgárosodás* might still be problematic, but this was the new reality.[9] Conspicuous inequalities emerged within the countryside; but the gap between countryside and town, narrowing in any case as the result of migration and socialist industrialization, ceased to be the gulf that it had been in the pre-socialist decades. This can be theorized as the transcendence of the *népi-urbánus* opposition by new forms of citizenship. The peasantry, even in *tanya*-dominated zones such as the Danube-Tisza interfluve, was now fully integrated and effectively extinguished. The post-peasants could participate fully in the entitlements of what I have elsewhere termed "socialist civilization."[10]

Of course, there were limits to this paradoxical realization of populist aspirations. The promotors of the "agrarian lobby" had to pay lip service to socialism; they were not free to form their own political party. But the influence of a populist-socialist synthesis became pervasive in the last decades of socialism. It was not limited to the provinces and the transformation of

---

8 Nigel Swain, *Collective Farms Which Work?* (Cambridge University Press 1985); Zsuzsanna Varga, *The Hungarian Agricultural Miracle? Sovietization and Americanization in a Communist Country* (Rowman & Littlefield 2021). Chris Hann, *Tázlár: a village in Hungary* (Cambridge University Press 1980).

9 Szelényi (n 2).

10 Chris Hann "Backwardness revisited: time, space and civilization in rural Eastern Europe" (2015) 57 *Comparative Studies in Society and History* 881–911.

agriculture, though this was where continuities with the critical sociography of the pre-socialist era were most obvious. The new freedoms were well illustrated by the revival of the monograph series *Magyarország felfedezése* in 1970. Ferenc Erdei himself contributed a monograph on Szeged and its hinterland.[11] Iván Boldizsár joined like-minded luminaries of the *népi* tradition on the Editorial Board. Most authors continued to focus on the countryside, but critique now extended to a broad range of topics, from urban squalor to the world of elite sportsmen. Contributing authors highlighted the costs of socialist transition, including shadow dimensions of the new market economy, new forms of hierarchy (e.g., as evident in Communist Party officials' love of hunting), and pathologies such as alcoholism. One outstanding example of the genre in its socialist form was Tibor Zám's *Bács-Kiskunból jövök*, which documented shady phenomena of the interfluve far better than my own monograph about Tázlár, published a few years later.[12]

Among more academic analyses of rural transformation, Tibor Simó investigated the settlement of Tard, the subject of Szabó's first study in 1936. The sociologist, an employee of a research institute of the Central Committee of the Hungarian Socialist Workers' Party, found that it had become a prosperous community thanks to the socialist transformation of agriculture. This work was later scathingly reviewed by László Siklós, who also drew attention to the brevity of Szabó's original fieldwork (a mere four weeks) and his heavy reliance on assistance from a village schoolteacher.[13] I doubt that Simó's work was ever read by Zoltán Szabó, who retired from Radio Free Europe in 1979 and died at his home in Brittany in 1984. Szabó devoted his retirement years to preparing the disparate corpus of manuscripts by István Bibó for publication. They did not meet again after 1949. By the 1980s it was possible to debate Bibó's work openly and the inauguration of the Kollégium that bears his name in 1983 was indicative of the new climate.

But the influence of populist imaginaries went much further. In the urban sphere, from the time of my arrival in 1975 it was impossible to overlook the popularity of the *táncház* movement. This has been studied

---

11 Ferenc Erdei, *Város és vidéke* (Szépírodalmi 1971).

12 Tibor Zám, *Bács-Kiskunból jövök* (Szépírodalmi 1973). See also by the same author *Tanyabejáró. Szociográfiai tanulmányok* (Forrás Könyvek 1977).

13 László Siklós, "Újabb tardi helyzet" *Siklós László író honlapja* (2013), <http://www.sikloslaszlo.hu/ujabb-tardi-helyzet> accessed July 20, 2023.

in depth by U.S. anthropologist Mary Taylor.[14] Building on the work of Iván Vitányi, she shows how socialist cultural managers developed ideals of "cultivation" that had their roots in much older national attachments and aspirations. Contemporary Western pop music was also immensely influential in Hungary in those years. But through music and dance, large numbers of mainly young people found themselves attracted by a culture that was distinctive, with which they could identify historically. The triumph was complete when artists such as *Muzsikás* achieved global recognition in the realm of "world music." In this way, socialist cultural managers could show themselves to be patriotically cultivating the traditions of their small nation, but always in the interests of a larger humanity. *Népi* traditions were predictably prominent in heritagization processes, but also in less visible ways in curricula and the organization of leisure time. Some of the families I knew in Tázlár who invested heavily in raising pigs because this was the most profitable sector of the household economy also devoted time and energy to producing embroidery and lace in styles considered to be traditional.

This pervasive embracing of the *népi* can be theorized as a reaction to the breakneck trends of socialist civilization that were transforming town and countryside alike. The symbiotic relationship between communism and populism was not free of political edge. While critique was tolerated, certain populist authors were apparently excluded from consideration for the *Magyarország felfedezése* series for political reasons (notably Sándor Csóori). The socialist regime did not have an easy relationship with Ceauşescu's Romania, and the support extended to cultural traits concentrated among the Hungarian minority of Transylvania risked provoking a larger neighbor and fanning nationalist flames at home. At the very end of his life, my former boss at the Lapkiadó Vállalat Iván Boldizsár commented on this delicate balancing act and appeared to welcome the evocations of national sentiment that were becoming ever more conspicuous in the public sphere.[15]

---

14 Mary N. Taylor, *Movement of the People. Hungarian Folk Dance, Populism, and Citizenship* (Indiana University Press 2021).

15 Iván Boldizsár, "The past as prologue" (1988) 112 *New Hungarian Quarterly* 3–7.

1.3 Postsocialism

It was not difficult to detect tensions between town and countryside, between *urbánus* and *népi*, in the campaigning ahead of the democratic elections of 1990. The two main forces opposing the reformed Communist Party (henceforth known as the Hungarian Socialist Party) were the Hungarian Democratic Forum and the Alliance of Free Democrats, whose strongholds lay in the countryside and town respectively. Throughout the 1990s the revived Independent Smallholders' Party was a force to be reckoned with. In the new century, all of these parties have disappeared. The *népi* camp has been dominated by the Fidesz party led by Viktor Orbán, in power since 2010 in coalition with the Christian Democrats. The opposition remains fragmented, and unification efforts failed miserably in the election of 2022.

The monograph series *Magyarország felfedezése* seems to have gradually lost its way in the new climate. The financial support previously guaranteed by a state publisher was no longer available. The Editorial Board was replaced by a new *Kuratórium*, but chaotic shifts from one publisher to another reflected the general chaos of the 1990s. This impacted on quality, since many potential authors found their own existential security under threat in this period. Sociography had always been something of a gray zone somewhere between journalism and academic social science. Some thought it should be consolidated in the guise of cultural anthropology. There is indeed overlap in interests and methods, but efforts to strengthen new forms of anthropology have not been very successful institutionally. I have not examined recent publications in the series but the homepage gives a dispiriting impression.[16] With public media under the control of a single party, the need for critical sociography is greater than ever. But who is to create and finance such a sociography in traditional forms in a brave new world in which tweets and blogs on independent internet portals offer the only opportunities to dissent from the state's narrative? The ruling party funds institutes to research every aspect of *magyarság* but it has no interest in funding an institute that might fund, say, a new generation of studies of

---

16 For a recent wide-ranging assessment of the genre into the twenty-first century and discussion of its prospects, published in the celebrated series and edited by the president of the *Kurátorium*, see Pál Péter Tóth (ed.), *A magyar szociográfia a 20-21. században* (Gondolat 2018).

coping strategies on the Danube-Tisza interfluve, or in the village of Tard. Such investigations would show that decollectivization had social as well as economic costs. It has led to new forms of hierarchy (e.g., the dependencies resulting from *közmunka* schemes), and to the weakening of family ties caused by high rates of migration to the West.

The new populists exercise a monopoly over the state that is comparable to that exercised by the Hungarian Socialist Workers' Party before 1989. The ideological initiative was seized by Orbán after his defeat in 2002, when he made the notorious claim that "the nation cannot be in opposition." Later assertions concerning "illiberal democracy" have fostered his reputation among liberals at home and abroad as a populist who does not respect the principles of a pluralist democracy, not to mention the control he has consolidated over the institutions of the judiciary, education, and the media. In countless provocations, such as his handling of migration his disdain for liberal elites in Brussels and Berlin, and his friendship with Vladimir Putin, Orbán has shown himself to be a maverick populist in that sense of the word that has become dominant in our age; he is a populist in the demagogic sense of Donald Trump rather than the democratic spirit of William Jennings Bryan or the Eastern European *narodniky* of an earlier age.[17]

Orbán knows how to reach out to rural voters and sometimes does so in very deliberate ways. The vast schemes of public works implemented in the 2020s were designed to buttress support at village level and I think they were successful in doing so for solid material reasons. In an era in which the traditional peasant pigsticking has become infrequent (since it is so much cheaper and easier to buy the products from a German-owned supermarket chain), Orbán demonstrates that he knows how to engender nostalgia for this tradition through astute videos available at his homepage. Viktor is a small-town kid, just like anyone else. As befits a politician who read Gramsci in his student years, he understands the importance of ideas, of creating new forms of hegemony. The rhetoric of national cooperation and putting the nation first is all designed to further this anti-pluralist goal.

---

17 The best account of Orbán and his system of "national cooperation" known to me is Stefano Bottoni, *A hatalom megszállottja; Orbán Viktor Magyarországa* (Magyar Hang 2023).

To theorize this new hegemony, I would follow Mary Taylor and place the new populism in the context of the accelerating globalization of the neoliberal decades. If the original *táncház* movement can be understood in the context of a socialist modernity that left millions fearful of homogenizing identity loss, that danger appears even greater in the disembedded capitalist global economy when your countrymen are free to move elsewhere and there is no protection against the economic power of corporations and banks based in the West. In these conditions, *népies* heritagization no longer suffices and *populista* currents become dangerous, undermining rule of law both at home and in the context of the EU. Meanwhile, small numbers of oppositionist intellectuals look back to Zoltán Szabó and István Bibó as exemplars of a liberal-democratic alternative.

1.4 Conclusion

There is something odd about a social anthropologist dabbling in history, especially the history of literature and ideas. I have explained why, during my work in the late socialist decades, I had no interest either in scholarly projects to classify the reformed socialist economy in Western neo-Marxist terms, or in celebrations of István Bibó. I don't think the name Bibó was known at all in Tázlár, though he has family roots in the petty gentry (*köznemes*) Calvinist elites of neighboring Kiskunhalas. The name of Ferenc Erdei was known only to the chief accountant at the *szakszövetkezet*, who recalled listening to his forceful lectures in the 1960s as a student at the Karl Marx University of Economics. In his case, I was able to discuss the scientific work and learn from academic colleagues such as Mihály Sárkány in Budapest. My priorities at the time lay elsewhere—in ethnography. The only empirical components of this lecture have been the tangential references to Iván Boldizsár, who was my line-manager for a year, after I had processed my Tázlár data.[18]

---

18 I experienced Boldizsár as an aloof employer, whose appearances in our offices on Rákóczi út were limited to key meetings before printers' deadlines. I was aware even at the time of his reputation as a man lacking personal integrity, always willing to put his journalistic talents to the service of power. He will not be remembered as a great writer. But his early commitment to populist causes, the risks he ran in the anti-Nazi resistance, abiding friendship with Zoltán Szabó, and consistent support for "liberal" reform initiatives in the last decades of his life suggest we might view him more charitably.

My limited reading focused not on dissident critique but more on contemporary journalism and the genre of sociography, which enjoyed a notable revival in the 1970s. I became aware of the origins of this genre in the pre-socialist years, but I failed to notice changing cultural forms of populism under socialism. In the populist political climate of the new century, it is instructive to connect the three phases: an emancipatory literary movement, a symbiotic relationship with socialist modernity, and an anti-pluralist reaction to neoliberal capitalist globalization. I follow the lead of Ernest Gellner in analyzing the history of ideas and ideologies with reference to material contexts, both economic and political. It is never enough to evaluate the work of intellectuals with reference only to their intellectual contexts. In the case of Hungarian populism, the broader historical context is a trajectory of economic backwardness on the periphery of Europe; this was followed by four decades of socialist transformation, in the course of which the emancipatory developmental agendas of the original populists were largely implemented; in the phase of renewed peripherality since 1990, politicians abuse populist legacies to curtail pluralism and construct new hierarchies while critical intellectuals struggle to have an impact outside of their own narrow circles.

Bibliography

Boldizsár I., *A gazdag parasztok országa* (Franklin 1940).

——— *Keser-édes* (Magvető 1987).

——— "The past as prologue." (1988) 112 *New Hungarian Quarterly* 3–7.

Bottoni S., *A hatalom megszállottja; Orbán Viktor Magyarországa* (Magyar Hang 2023).

Borbándi G., *Der ungarische Populismus* (Hase & Koehler 1976).

Erdei F., *Futóhomok* (Athenaeum 1937).

——— *Város és vidéke* (Szépirodalmi 1971).

Hann C., Tázlár: A village in Hungary (Cambridge UP 1980).

——— "Backwardness revisited: time, space and civilization in rural Eastern Europe" (2015) 57 *Comparative Studies in Society and History* 881.

Hofer T., "Anthropologists and native ethnographers in Central European villages. Comparative notes on the professional personality of two disciplines" (1968) 9 *Current Anthropology* 311.

Noszkai G., 2009-10. "Bibó István és Szabó Zoltán barátságának története"(Parts 1 and 2) (2009–10) 14–15 *Beszélő.*

Siklós L., "Újabb tardi helyzet" (2013) *Siklós László író honlapja* <http://www.sikloslaszlo.hu/ujabb-tardi-helyzet/> accessed July 20, 2023.

Swain N., Collective Farms Which Work? (Cambridge UP 1985).

Szelényi I., Socialist Entrepreneurs. Embourgeosisement in Rural Hungary (University of Wisconsin Press 1986).

Taylor M. N., Movement of the People. Hungarian Folk Dance, Populism, and Citizenship. (Indiana University Press 2021).

Tóth P. P., *A magyar szociográfia a 20-21. században* (Gondolat 2018).

Varga Zs, The Hungarian Agricultural Miracle? Sovietization and Americanization in a Communist Country (Rowman & Littlefield 2021).

Zám T., *Bács-Kiskunból jövök* (Szépirodalmi 1973).

——— *Tanyabejáró. Szociográfiai tanulmányok* (Forrás Könyvek 1977).

Studying Central European Laws Through the Legrand Perspective: Using the Negative to Approach the Different

*Balázs Fekete**

ABSTRACT
Balázs Fekete introduces Pierre Legrand's approach to comparative legal studies, which challenges the orthodox, positivist methodology. He argues that Central European legal studies often neglect the cultural and social contexts of legal phenomena. Fekete advocates for a more nuanced understanding of legal transplants and the role of local culture in shaping legal norms.

Keywords: comparative law, negative comparative law, Pierre Legrand, Central European legal studies

> [...] I was always convinced that Europe not only means Western Europe—France, Great Britain, the Federal Republic of Germany, Italy etc.—but the so-called "other Europe," Central East Europe, too; which was a forgotten and oppressed, but sometimes a frightening and rejectable Europe. This division, rejection and conscious distancing from the central and eastern part of Europe has primarily been blamed on Stalinism, but a part of this responsibility also goes to the Western World, being full of prejudices [...][1]

2.1 Negative Comparative Law: a new sensitivity and affection

Pierre Legrand has been advocating a radically different approach to comparative legal studies among the comparatist-at-law scholarly community for some time. In essence, contemporary comparative law discourse is dominated by an orthodox approach, which has a hegemonic character.[2] However, in the shadow and at the periphery of this orthodox comparative law understanding, some divergent—one could say heretical or unorthodox—ideas on comparative law also exist, and have always existed.[3] Although their relevance

---

* Professor and Department Chair, ELTE Faculty of Law Department of Legal and Social Theory Senior Research Fellow, Institute for Legal Studies, ELTE Centre for Social Sciences, Budapest.

1 Claudio Magris, "Utószó a magyar kiadáshoz" in Claudio Magris, *Duna* (Európa 1992) 439. Translated by the author.

2 Pierre Legrand, *Negative Comparative Law* (CUP 2022) 19–21.

3 Cf ibid. 47–103.

is obvious, they are however fragmented and also occupy a marginal place in the ongoing discourse, if any. The main goals in Legrand's forays into comparative law methodology, from abstract questions of epistemology to the proper translation of foreign legal sources, is therefore to highlight some components of this much less-known and less-valued heterodoxy. In addition, he also submits that the construction of a precise and accurate background theory to anchor comparative legal studies based on these kinds of insights is neither possible nor a key requirement, since, in its post-positivist era,[4] legal scholarship no longer needs it anymore. As such, contrary to all these uncertainties, this drastically different orientation is capable of revealing new and provocative approaches to the classic themes by challenging (or even negating) them on epistemological or other grounds. Legrand is deeply convinced of the need to rethink and renew the toolkit of traditional comparative law, with special regard to its epistemological basis and implied ethical commitments, and he presents non-mainstream points that must play a crucial role in this transformation process.[5]

This essay serves to back this claim by using the examples of some comparative law enterprises focusing on Central European[6] legal issues. It will

---

4 Cf ibid. 12–13.

5 The task to summarize and explain all the main points of Legrand's understanding of comparative legal studies would be too ambitious for this short essay. If the reader is interested in these, they may consult Legrand's latest books [Legrand (n 2) or Pierre Legrand, *Comparative Law and the Task of Negative Critique* (Routledge 2023) and perhaps my review essay on Legrand's *Negative Comparative Law* (Balázs Fekete, "The Power of Negative: Notes on Pierre Legrand's Negative Comparative Law" [2023] 18 *Journal of Comparative Law* 379).

6 Here, in this essay, I use the term "Central Europe" in a conventional geographical sense. This term covers the countries in between Germany and Belarus and Ukraine, and this area is delimited by the Balkans from the south. The Baltics may also be included. I'm aware of the various possible historical and political counterarguments against this simplified use of the term, but for the idea of this essay this approach seems to suit well. In addition, as a Central European scholar I also share the conviction that this region has certain distinctive features that made it a unique European historical region as compared to Western Europe, The Balkans, Scandinavia or the Mediterranean. On Central Europe as a historical region, see Jenő Szűcs's, George Schöpflin's, or László Péter's classic pieces (Jenő Szűcs, "The Three Historical Regions of Europe: An Outline" [1983] 29 *Acta Historica Academiae Scientiarum Hungaricae* 131; George Schöpflin, "The Political Traditions of Eastern Europe" [1990] 119 *Daedalus* 55; László Péter, "Central Europe and Its Reading into the Past" [1999] 6 *European Review of History* 101).

be argued that although research on Central European laws has been growing continuously, or even blooming, these studies still represent a narrow, prominently de-contextualized orientation, which disregards other important factors that play a key role in gaining an in-depth, or thick understanding.[7] Hence, the explanations provided by—let me use this term—the "new Central European legal studies" suffer from serious deficiencies, even though they offer discussions at a high academic level of various legal phenomena from a positivistic perspective. For example, most of them put their focus on strict legal issues, thereby separating the legal phenomenon from its natural context(s), resulting in a strong social and cultural neglect that characterizes them. Furthermore, they also tend to neglect some elementary ethical commitments that are implied by the very nature of using the comparative method for studying legal phenomena. Third, even though their authors recognize the role of legal transplants in the transformation of the legal orders of the Central European countries, most of them share a very schematic view on this process, which has led them to weaker conclusions.

2.2 "New Central European legal studies": two examples ...

We are all aware that "Central European law" has become a major subject of scholarly projects having a comparative scope these days.[8] This is apparent with regard to constitutional law issues (just check the literature on the ongoing Hungarian-Polish rule-of-law crisis, for example), but the private laws of the region also underwent a remarkable transformation over the last ten years. For instance, new Civil Codes were enacted in Romania in 2009

7 Cf Clifford Geertz, "Thick Description: Toward an Interpretive Theory of Culture" in Clifford Geertz, *The Interpretation of Cultures* (Basic Books 2017) 3.

8 Sometimes numbers can be very telling. If someone tries to have a look on the frequency of the appearance of the expressions: "rule of law" AND Hungary and "rule of law" AND Poland in the search engine of the Heinonline law journal library, narrowed down to articles exclusively, they will find a clear difference as between the periods 1990–2009 and 2010–23. From 1990 to 2009, these two expressions are listed 4158 (Hungary) and 5085 (Poland) times, while, from 2010 to 2023, their mentions in the texts of articles grew significantly: 7214 (Hungary) and 8220 (Poland). This well illustrates how scholarly interest in the region's legal developments has continuously been growing from the 2010s.

and Hungary in 2013. Contemporary Central Europe has therefore been an ideal place for carrying out comparative law investigations, as the various changes in the post-1989 constitutional and private law setting attracted a lot of attention from outside. In addition, as the constitutional transformation in countries like Hungary or Poland openly deviated from or tried to challenge the post-transitional regional liberal-democratic consensus—the former Socialist countries would follow the Western social, political, and legal patterns in order to return to the European community[9]—politics also motivated legal and other scholars to study the transformation of the regional legal orders.

In this essay I would like to pick two specific volumes as, for me, they demonstrate well what these "new Central European legal studies" look like. The first one is the volume "Comparative Constitutionalism in Central Europe"[10] edited by two Hungarian academics, Lóránt Csink and László Trócsányi, while the second is the monograph "European Legal Cultures in Transition,"[11] written by Åse B. Grødeland and William L. Miller. At the very first sight, these two books cannot be further from each other. One of them provides a meticulous comparison of the constitutional law provisions of Central Europe and the former Yugoslavia's successor states, while the other discusses some features of a few European legal cultures, including certain Central and East European ones, such as those of Bulgaria, Poland and Ukraine along with Norway and the United Kingdom. In addition, one was written by leading Western socio-legal scholars with a strong institutional background, while the editors of the other are Central Europeans and they are affiliated to a newly—in 2019—founded and government-backed comparative law institute in Budapest. The volume focusing on comparative constitutionalism applies to a strictly legalistic perspective and vocabulary, while, on the other hand, the volume discussing some European legal cultures

---

9 Cf Reinhard Heinisch, "Returning to Europe and the Rise of Europragmatism" in Irina Livezeanu and Árpád von Klimó (eds), *The Routledge History of East Central Europe since* 1700 (Routledge 2020) 415–29.

10 Lóránt Csink and László Trócsányi (eds), Comparative Constitutionalism in Central Europe. Analysis on Certain Central and Eastern European Countries (Central European Academic Publishing 2022).

11 Åse B. Grødeland and William L. Miller, *European Legal Cultures in Transition* (CUP 2015).

subscribes to the socio-legal studies tradition. Even so, let me argue for this point; on a meta-level, these volumes share those common problems that are able to connect them, regardless of all the above-mentioned differences. Moreover, this essay is to expose these meta-points and to provide a criticism that can contribute to a more refined methodological approach to the legal orders in Central Europe.

2.3 "New Central European legal studies": ... and their critique

2.3.1 The importance of "meta": methodological criticism

So, how can the Legrand perspective be applied to discussing these two books and the comparative law vision they represent? Two possibilities seem to be almost self-evident. First, the Legrand standpoint may help to expose some general deficiencies of this vision from a critical or negative angle. Second, as this region has been a constant object of legal transfers and transplants coming from the West since the start of the political and legal transition in 1989, the Legrand perspective can also contribute to a better understanding of these dynamics and their partial misrepresentation by both of these books.

As a starting point, so from a general perspective, it has to be recognized that these two books are strongly related to the conventional, Zweigert-Kötz inspired positivist comparative law legacy.[12] In other words, they endorse the approach of the well-known manual when framing their projects. As a striking example Trócsányi, one of the editors of the Central European comparative constitutionalism volume, makes this endorsement explicit in his foreword:

> As Konrad Zweigert famously argued, "the basic methodological principle of all comparative law is that of functionality." Accordingly, legal provisions shall be analysed and compared within the social and economic context in which they prevail, and the process of comparison shall answer the question of how this legal provision works.[13]

---

[12] For a discussion of the Zweigert-Kötz inspired approach see: Mathias Siems, *Comparative Law* (CUP 2014) 13–40, Geoffrey Samuel, *An Introduction to Comparative Law Theory and Method* (Hart 2014) 63–78 and also Legrand (n 2) 60–103 (revealing all the main points through deconstruction).

[13] László Trócsányi, "Foreword" in Csink and Trócsányi (eds) (n 10) 16.

To some extent perhaps surprisingly (since it is a comparison of legal cultures and not a comparative analysis of specific legal provisions), the methodological chapter of the Grødeland-Miller book also invokes the authority of the Zweigert-Kötz approach to comparison in law through the application of one of its basic terms—legal family—and a direct reference to Kötz. This terminological choice implies the acceptance of the main presumptions of this strictly positivist theory. For example, it seems that the authors share the idea that the different national legal orders can be grouped into broader units, as they share common features besides the superficial differences, or that the main goal of comparison of laws is to reveal the similarities of legal orders.[14] In addition, in the eyes of the authors, their choice of legal cultures to compare—a key component of any comparative enterprise in law—is partly justified by the simple fact that they "belong to different legal families."[15] Thus, although the Grødeland-Miller monograph addresses the study of various legal cultures in Europe, its fundamental decision on the selection of legal cultures it compares is decisively influenced by the Zweigert-Kötz approach.

These two examples therefore suggest that comparative studies of Central European legal orders have still been under the influence of the "orthodox" understanding of comparative law. This has further implications, too. First of all, it leads to a rather similar narrative strategy of discussing the legal phenomena (whether a constitutional law provision or a specific feature of mass attitude toward law) in these works. In other words, the comparative constitutionalism manual mostly focuses on specific legal provisions, it generally discusses their history (predominantly in a narrow, descriptive and linear sense) and then it scrutinizes their phrasing and relation to case law, if any. If comparison is also on the map of this piece, this most commonly means a juxtaposition of the analyzed law-texts, and some textual similarities

[14] The conclusion of Grødeland and Miller clearly reveals their endorsement of the "Zweigert-Kötz's fascination with similarity." Having compared and analyzed public attitudes toward the law in Western and Eastern European countries from manifold aspects, they conclude, in a rather straightforward manner that "The most important finding from our country comparisons is that legal outsiders and insiders across Europe have fairly similar attitudes to "law in principle"—that is, what law is and what its role in society should be." Grødeland and Miller (n 11) 503.

[15] Grødeland and Miller (n 11) 9.

and differences are pointed out and analyzed by the author.[16] In addition, if possible, the findings of the study are also evaluated against some tenets of the relevant Western scholarship. To put it bluntly, no one denies that that these kinds of discussions are relevant and also have a scholarly value, but this approach can also be criticized from multiple aspects if we replace our conventional and habitual scholarly mindset, inspired by the Zweigert-Kötz stream of thinking, with Legrand's unconventional glasses.

This narrative pattern, although in a more subtle way, also appears in Grødeland-Miller's monograph. The chapters of this otherwise very impressive volume mostly offer strict data analysis, meaning that the authors provide a really detailed presentation of data on various popular attitudes toward the law, then they discuss the differences between "some numbers" in the countries studied, after which they also compare them with each other. The focus group discussion excerpts have an illustrative role in this presentation; they help "to animate" the numbers to some extent by giving voice to the people behind the abstract and lonely numbers. However, the authors mostly stop at the juxtaposition and do not really try to explain their findings in a broader context, one leading to a thick understanding. That is, Grødeland-Miller's analyses can give us a good overview of the state of certain attitudes in these legal cultures, as measured by a questionnaire survey and refined by the findings of focus group discussions, and they also enable us to rank them with each other, but they do not help us in understanding the *mentalité*[17] behind the similarities and differences.

From a Legrand perspective, some further comments can be put forward as follows. Let me be clear at this point; these in no way invalidate the volumes' findings, but point out some meta-issues that would also have been worth taking into account. The consideration of these meta-issues may contribute to an epistemologically more appropriate discussion, and this may pave the way to an understanding that would lead further than a detailed description.

First, it seems to be evident that these volumes and their authors are unaware that their work can never be a complete description of a foreign

[16] See, for example: Attila Horváth, "The Executive Power" in Csink and Trócsányi (eds) (n 10) 293–318.

[17] For details, see: Pierre Legrand, "European Legal Systems Are Not Converging" (1996) 45 *ICLQ* 52, 60–4.

law or a foreign legal culture—in our case, some Central European legal provisions or popular attitudes toward the law—but only give an interpretation based on their representation of the given issue. Legrand convincingly argues that, since all comparatists-at law are acclimatized in their own general and legal culture, as the foreign legal phenomena studied always represents foreignness, by its very quality, no comparatists can therefore, be able to understand, in an epistemological sense, the foreign legal phenomenon completely. The comparative discussion and analysis are therefore always distorted or manipulated—specifically, encultured persons discuss encultured legal phenomena differently—so they cannot achieve epistemological objectivity, but they discuss only re-presentations of the phenomenon according to the given comparatist's own world view.[18]

This fundamental problem of comparative law scholarship obviously cannot be solved, but it can be made explicit, by pointing out the limits of a given comparative law enterprise. As such, some words on the cultural and professional limitations of the research behind these volumes would have been welcomed, in the introductions at least. In addition, the awareness of this epistemological issue—put in a nutshell, that the Self will never be able to reach the Other[19]—could have seriously contributed to the analytical discussions of these books by softening their tones and making them more empathic toward differences. In conclusion, the validity of all their findings is necessarily constrained by epistemological concerns. Perhaps their findings are more limited than their authors considered them to be.

Second, it seems to be glaringly obvious that these books, in some cases, ignore both the cultural and political background of the legal phenomena studied. It seems that, for these scholars, Central European legal provisions and legal attitudes exist in isolation and they have no relationship to their broader context, including politics and general culture. If one accepts that law-texts are more than simple printed texts of legal provisions, as they also reflect the culture that produced them and they contain various "cultural traces,"[20] then such a discussion, that deprives legal provisions from their cultural context, can have only limited validity. In addition, the discussion of

18 Legrand (n 2) 377–83.
19 Ibid. 9.
20 Ibid. 209–10.

constitutional law provisions without bringing into play the political context is almost senseless if one would like to know more than simply how these norms are phrased. The same points apply to a de-cultured and predominantly ahistorical discussion of attitudes toward law, which strictly focuses on data analysis, I think. These two books can therefore only offer limited vision of their subject matters. Their visions are predominantly positivistic and lay claim to objectivity, as they separate the subject studied from its cultural context and it leads to an "understanding" in which the encultured nature of the legal provisions and public legal attitudes are and will be almost invisible to most of the authors and readers.

The only exception from this reluctance to take into account cultural points is the historical interest, as the comparative constitutionalism volume presents the constitutional history of each Central European and Balkan country studied. The Grødeland-Miller volume also refers to certain historical points, for example, the legacy of the communist past on the formation of popular attitudes toward law. Interestingly, Grødeland and Miller mostly use historical references when they try to explain how Eastern popular attitudes differ from the Western mentality.[21] However, these historical introductions to country-specific constitutional histories in the comparative constitutionalism volume are rather schematic, as they only provide a linear and descriptive discussion of relevant events and legal documents in most cases[22] and they do not dig deeply into the social and political history of the given country. In comparison, the historical references in Grødeland-Miller's work seem mostly superficial and do not suggest that the authors have a comprehensive sense of how the history of Central and East Europe makes it a unique region in Europe. As such, although these historical components of these books are definitely relevant, and this should be acknowledged, they are not really capable of expanding the interpretive room of the discussions toward a more refined and complete outlook.

---

21 Cf for example Grødeland and Miller (n 11) 31–3, 187–9, 193, 207.

22 An exception from this general orientation is Manuel Gutan's paper on Romania's modern legal history. The author focuses on the historical and political dynamics behind the main influences shaping Romanian constitutional identity. See Manuel Gutan, "Romanian Constitutional Identity in Historical Context" in Csink and Trócsányi (eds) (n 10) 109–28.

Third, it is also quite apparent that most authors overlook one of their ethical commitments, at least partly. The principle of charitable interpretation—meaning that a legal phenomenon has to be interpreted as empathically as possible and with maximum consideration for the inherent epistemological limitations of any comparative endeavors—seems to play a very limited role in their work. In many cases, the authors are apparently satisfied with scratching the surface instead of attempting to study the phenomena, comparing them as sensitively as possible. Most of the findings therefore remain rather schematic and seem to strengthen the conventional wisdom instead of coming up with new points and ideas that would be able to refine or enrich the state of the art on Central and East European law and legal cultures.

A Legrand-inspired critical discussion of these two books' methodological premises shows one point clearly. The implementation of certain components of Legrand's approach to "New Central European legal studies" would definitely be able to bring new and vibrant colors into this discourse in place of its recent, rather depressing, dull and gray character. And the more colorful a picture is, the more likely it will inspire others to elaborate on it.

2.3.2 For a more refined understanding of legal transplants

The critical discussion of the two books earlier, and the stream of "New Central European legal studies" cannot be complete without referring to the issue of legal transplants. It is no exaggeration to say that the post-1989 history of Central and East Europe is also the history of legal transplants. It is beyond doubt that this region, as broadly understood as possible, has been a primary target for legal exports from the beginning of the post-socialist political transition process. Constitutions, private codes, anti-discrimination laws, and competition laws were renewed or completely remade in the 1990s and the major source of inspiration was definitely "Western Law," or "Western Legal Tradition" as such.[23] In addition, the aspirations of EU accession also motivated these countries to subscribe to existing Western European legal standards in order to harmonize their legal orders with the existing *acquis communautaire*. Legal transplantation has therefore been a main driver in the

---

[23] Gianmaria Ajani, "By Chance and Prestige: Legal Transplants in Russia and Eastern Europe" (1995) 43 *The American Journal of Comparative Law* 93.

last decades' regional legal developments, and this process has been studied according to positivist and law-text oriented premises.[24]

However, here Legrand also offers a valuable perspective that may help to open a new horizon for studying this phenomenon using comparative means, and this is not a complete denial of the possibility of legal transplantation, which is repeatedly associated with Legrand's name.[25] He argues that, when discussing globalization as an engine of world-wide legal development, the term "glocalization" may be a more apt description of what has been happening when legal models are transplanted from one country or region to another one. The essence of "glocalization" is the simple fact that outsider legal norms—implying a different cultural background—can only become effective in the importing legal order, at least to some extent, if they adapt themselves to the context, the local, to which they arrive. That is, the implementation of outsider—so to say global or Western—norms is strongly dependent on the local conditions, including the uniqueness of local culture, and these norms must adapt to them in order to have some social impact as desired by the lawmakers. Therefore, it is argued by Legrand, one cannot talk about global constitutionalism or universal human rights norms, but only about their "glocalized" versions, partly preserving the global content, mostly in their phrasing, but also partly transformed through their everyday application by the local administration and judiciary.[26]

It would be fascinating to learn more about how the glocalization of Western European legal models happened in this region. What is the reality behind these well-sounding, and many times celebrated, regional transplantation attempts? I am deeply convinced that Legrand's perspective can help in this case and not only because his ideas on glocalization could inspire the formulation of these questions, but because his culturalist and hermeneutical toolbox is also able to offer some radically new tools at this field. For instance, I am pretty sure that local external legal cultures—that is, mass attitudes to law—has had a great impact on the everyday functioning of these

---

24 See, for example: Dimiter Toshkov, "Compliance with EU Law in Central and Eastern Europe the Disaster that Didn't Happen (Yet)" (2012) *L'Europe en formation* 91.

25 Pierre Legrand, "The Impossibility of 'Legal Transplants'" (1997) 4 *Maastricht Journal of European and Comparative Law* 111.

26 Legrand (n 2) 120–8.

norms. In our latest study, for example, we found that the pervasive legal alienation characterizing the Hungarian legal culture has a strong impact on legal mobilization and this seriously affect the role that rights may play in ordinary disputes.[27]

For example, if any kind of discrimination occurs, but the legal way of settlement does not seems to be attractive as there is a general skepticism toward the law and my fellows also have some disappointing stories about their failures when trying to find their "justice" in the maze of the justice system,[28] the fact that anti-discrimination laws in a given country meet the highest Western standards, at least from a black-letter law perspective, can only be of questionable value, if any. In addition, the idea that law is an instrument in the hands of the government, going back to eighteenth-century modernization efforts,[29] is also an important factor when explaining why governments in this region may have a different attitude toward EU law commitments than their Western counterparts. Moreover, it can be easy to continue this line by adding other factors—for example, the pervasiveness of the autocratic political tradition,[30] the general lack of institutional trust as compared to Western Europe[31]—that can contribute to emergence of "glocalized" norms in the region. All in all, the phenomenon of glocalization seems to have a crucial relevance when someone wants to have an empathic and charitable understanding of the regional failures and success of legal transplantation.

---

27 Balázs Fekete, Attila Bartha, György Gajduschek, and Fruzsina Gulya, "Rights Consciousness in Hungary and Some Comparative Remarks. Could an Increasing Level of Rights Consciousness Challenge the Autocratic Tradition?" (2022) 47 *Review of Central and East European Law* 220.

28 Balázs Fekete, "Rights Consciousness in Hungary. What is Behind the Numbers? Lessons of a Focus Group Study" in Ulrike Schultz, David Nelken, Roger Cotterrell, and Håkan Hydén (eds), *Combining the Legal and the Social in Sociology of Law: An Homage to Reza Banakar* (Hart 2023) 173–88.

29 Péter László, "Autokrácia Kelet-Európában" in Péter László, *Az Elbától keletre* (Osiris 1998) 40–1.

30 ibid. 4–56.

31 Sajó András, "Az állam működési zavarainak társadalmi újratermelése" (2008) 55 *Közgazdasági Szemle* 690.

2.4 Central European laws: the different within

Although some of Legrand's findings may be too radical for most comparatists-at-law, their epistemological and methodological relevance cannot be denied, as the philosophical background of social sciences has drastically changed in the last decades (just think of terms like "hermeneutics," "postmodern," "deconstruction," or "decoloniality"). From the aspect of studying Central European laws and legal cultures, they are especially relevant as they help to develop a critical attitude toward the ongoing, dominant discourse. Obviously, the points of this critical discourse are to be debated, too, but one lesson is clear: the settled methodology of comparative law enterprises is clearly not enough to come up with a proper picture of legal developments in the Central European region. As extra-legal factors—history, politics and social developments—play a key role in establishing the uniqueness of these legal orders—*they make* a *difference*—as compared to their Western counterparts, only such approaches that are able to look beyond the horizon of conventional comparative law methodologies can be rewarding. Hence, in the case of Central European legal studies, criticism is primarily not to deny, nor negate previous findings, but to open up new perspectives that are able to deal with *the different,* the peripheral—at least from the Western, so the central perspective—in a more suitable and more charitable way.

Bibliography

Ajani G., "By Chance and Prestige: Legal Transplants in Russia and Eastern Europe" (1995) 43 *The American Journal of Comparative Law* 93.

Csink L. and Trócsányi L., (eds), *Comparative Constitutionalism in Central Europe. Analysis on Certain Central and Eastern European Countries* (Central European Academic Publishing 2022).

Fekete B., "Rights Consciousness in Hungary. What is Behind the Numbers? Lessons of a Focus Group Study" in Schultz U., Nelken D., Cotterrell R. and Hydén H. (eds), *Combining the Legal and the Social in Sociology of Law: An Homage to Reza Banakar* (Hart 2023) 173–88.

Fekete B., Bartha A., Gajduschek G. and Gulya F., "Rights Consciousness in Hungary and Some Comparative Remarks. Could an Increasing Level of Rights Consciousness Challenge the Autocratic Tradition?" (2022) 47 *Review of Central and East European Law* 220.

Geertz C., "Thick Description: Toward an Interpretive Theory of Culture" in Geertz C., *The Interpretation of Cultures* (Basic Books 2017) 3.

Grødeland Å. B. and Miller W. L., *European Legal Cultures in Transition* (CUP 2015).

Heinisch R., "Returning to Europe and the Rise of Europragmatism" in Livezeanu I and von Klimó Á (eds), *The Routledge History of East Central Europe since 1700* (Routledge 2020) 415–29.

Legrand P., *Comparative Law and the Task of Negative Critique* (Routledge 2023).

Legrand P., *Negative Comparative Law* (CUP 2022).

Legrand P., "European Legal Systems Are Not Converging" (1996) 45 *CLQ* 52.

Legrand P., "The Impossibility of 'Legal Transplants'" (1997) 4 *Maastricht Journal of European and Comparative Law* 111.

Magris C., "Utószó a magyar kiadáshoz" in Magris C, *Duna* (Európa 1992) 439.

Samuel G., *An Introduction to Comparative Law Theory and Method* (Hart 2014).

Schöpflin G., "The Political Traditions of Eastern Europe" (1990) 119 *Daedalus* 55.

Siems M., *Comparative Law* (CUP 2014).

Szűcs J., "The Three Historical Regions of Europe: An Outline" (1983) 29 *Acta Historica Academiae Scientiarum Hungaricae* 131.

Toshkov D., "Compliance with EU Law in Central and Eastern Europe the Disaster that Didn't Happen (Yet)' (2012) *L'Europe en formation* 91.

Looking for the Identity of the Constitutional Court of the Slovak Republic

Peter Čuroš

ABSTRACT
This chapter examines the constitutional identity of the Slovak Constitutional Court (SCC). It discusses the historical development of constitutional review in Czechoslovakia and Slovakia, highlighting the influence of the Austrian and German legal traditions. It analyzes the SCC's role in shaping the Slovak legal system, focusing on significant cases, arguing that the SCC struggles to find its identity.

Keywords: Slovak Constitutional Court, constitutional identity, Slovak constitutional identity

3.1 Introduction[1]

Constitutional identity is a multifaceted concept. It refers to the core principles, values, and fundamental features that define a nation's constitutional framework and underpin its legal and political system. It encapsulates the unique and intrinsic elements that make a particular constitution distinct from others. Constitutional identity represents the essence of a nation's self-understanding and its vision of governance. However, looking for such an identity might be difficult in the countries of the periphery. The peripheral legal systems were either cut off from their historical tradition or did not possess such a tradition. These systems are defined by absorbing legal institutions and norms that are not autonomous products of their legal order but transplanted from foreign legal systems. The primary reasons for such transplantation are their necessity for quick solutions that appeared successful in other countries or a dictate from the cultural hegemon within the region.

Despite the embeddedness of the constitutional judiciary in the CEE region, a constitutional court is a type of transplant that has not yet found its planned identity in the system of the Slovak Republic. In the Kelsenian hierarchical structure of norms, where a constitutional court is a guardian

1 The work presented in this article was supported by a research grant from the Polish National Science Centre (2021/41/B/HS5/01455).

of the constitutional norms that appear almost at the top of the pyramid, it is the constitutional court's role to interpret and mold the constitutional identity. However, the problem of the peripheral countries may be that even the constitutional judiciary is a kind of transplant that is looking for its role and cannot beat the normative power of the factual, which has already been in this system.

3.2 Normativist heritage mixed with casuistic approaches

Slovakia is no different from other Central and Eastern European countries in having strong faith in the omnipotence of regulation. Regulation, primarily legal, is considered an effective instrument for gaining control over behavior. Probably, the strong normative heritage from interwar Czechoslovakia,[2] molded by the mechanical formalist jurisprudence of state socialism,[3] has left its mark.

> During the socialist era, illusions controlled the way of thinking in socialist countries, resulting in a false reliance upon legislation or law. The illusion of the French Revolution was that the formulation of some general declaratory rules would be sufficient. In a similar way, after World War II, it was supposed that the central power could solve almost any problem in a short time.[4]

On the other hand, the casuistic approach in law, which is very popular in the peripheries, threatens consistency, creates potential subjectivity, and leads to unpredictable legal outcomes and a fragmented understanding of the law. Furthermore, the focus on individual cases usually hinders the development of broader legal principles and slows the evolution of legal standards in response to social changes. Doctrines need clarity when general principles are addressed. The downsides of formalism and casuistry can create a dangerous hybrid that allows particular interests into legislation and constitutional review.

---

2 Normativistic theories of František Weyr in Brno, or Hans Kelsen in Vienna.

3 Zdeněk Kühn: *The Judiciary in Central and Eastern Europe: Mechanical Jurisprudence in Transformation?* (Martinus Nijhoff Publishers, 2011) 116ff.

4 Attila Harmathy, 'Codification in a period of transition' (1998) 31 *U.C. Davis Law Review* 3 783, 785.

This leads to an outcome that resembles more the Schmittian version of the constitutional court rather than the Kelsenian one. Kelsen, a proponent of legal positivism, emphasized judicial supremacy and the importance of legal norms in a hierarchical structure, advocating for the constitutional court as the primary institution responsible for upholding constitutional law.[5] He viewed the court as the "Hüter der Verfassung," whose primary function was to ensure that all laws and governmental actions comply with constitutional provisions, interpreting the constitution independently of political influences to safeguard individual rights and maintain the rule of law.[6] In contrast, Schmitt critiqued this strictly legalistic approach, arguing that law and politics could not be neatly separated. He emphasized the necessity of political decisions, particularly during crises, and contended that the constitutional court's function must have extended beyond mere legal interpretation. According to Schmitt, the court should have navigated the political landscape and might need to act decisively to protect the state's integrity and stability, especially in exceptional circumstances. He posited that the court's authority derived from political realities and that the "sovereign" must have the power to suspend or reinterpret legal norms, placing the court in a more reactive role. The essential disagreement between the two thinkers lay in their views on the nature of the constitutional court's function. Kelsen prioritized an independent judiciary operating within a legal framework to promote stability and predictability. At the same time, Schmitt allowed flexibility and responsiveness to changing political circumstances. The difference was visible in Schmitt's dichotomy of friend-enemy when the aim of acting in the realm of political was to group with friends against the enemy.[7] In recent years, the activity of the Slovak Constitutional Court (SCC) reminds siding with a particular political spectrum to defeat the other.

As a result, the SCC is not "Hüter der Verfassung," but a guardian of the legal form. In such a formalist system, the Kelsenian hierarchical structure of law ends with the oblivion between good and bad laws. Therefore, the

---

5 Lars Vinx (ed and trs), *The Guardian of the Constitution: Hans Kelsen and Carl Schmitt on the Limits of Constitutional Law* (CUP 2015) 22.

6 Vinx (n 5) 79.

7 C Schmitt, *The Concept of the Political* (George Schwab tr, University of Chicago Press, 1996) 26.

child of Kelsen's theory—the protector of the constitution—cannot decide upon the dichotomy of good and bad law. The form of law will always limit it. Thus, the SCC protects any interest that the legal form enshrines. So, while, in general, we perceive the constitutional judiciary as a pro-democratic institution, this is not a necessary connection. This chapter presents several examples of how the situation may deteriorate when the constitutional court cannot find its proper position within the system of the constitutional order and serves as a tool of other interests, in the Slovak case of the judicial and political.

This chapter also elucidates 30 years of the development of the SCC. The Slovak example offers us one exceptional case study in which we can observe the development of the constitutional culture, the struggle between parliamentary and judicial interests, and, finally, attempts by particular players to acquire more power. When a constitutional court is portrayed as the guardian of the constitution, any interest that aspires for more influence wants the stamp of legitimacy from it. Therefore, the constitutional court has become the stamp-giver of legitimacy and a political tool for winning the argument.

The chapter is structured as follows. First, it sketches out the emergence of the SCC, its predecessor institutions, and previous experiences. Subsequently, the Court's relevance in establishing the state institutions is described. Several significant judgments made in the 1990s mirror the Court's important role. Finally, it is shown by five controversial landmark cases. The chapter ends with a summary and evaluation of the findings.

3.3 Short excurse to the history of constitutional review in Czechoslovakia

The SCC considers itself the successor to the Constitutional Court of the Czechoslovak Republic from the interwar years. However, this lineage was disrupted and intertwined with various institutions and ideas. The Czechoslovak Constitutional Court (CCC) and the Austrian Constitutional Court were among the first in Europe to conduct constitutional review. The CCC's primary role was to invalidate any laws contradicting the constitution or constitutional amendments.[8] Its mandate involved two forms of review: assessing

---

[8] Art. 1 and 2 of law on Constitution of Czechoslovak Republic no. 121/1920 Coll.

the substantive constitutionality of laws, ensuring their content complied with constitutional principles, and evaluating the formal constitutionality by checking adherence to prescribed legal procedures.[9]

Although, on paper, the CCC was intended to uphold democratic principles in the newly founded state, it did not meet the expectations set by the constitution's authors. In practice, the court was largely inactive for years, rendering decisions in only 46 cases throughout its existence, and it never resolved the two complaints about the primary agenda of the court on legal compliance with the constitution.[10]

A significant reason for such ineffectiveness was the seven-year delay in filling its judicial seats after the initial term ended on November 17, 1931. The National Assembly could only agree on appointing new judges on May 5, 1938. These new judges served only for a year before the CCC was dissolved following the Nazi occupation.

The CCC's ineffectiveness also stemmed from its dependence on motions to initiate proceedings. Only select bodies—the supreme court, election court, lower chamber of the National Assembly, and the assembly of Subcarpathian Ruthenia—could propose such motions, making it rare for a motion to proceed due to the stringent consensus required. Upon Czechoslovakia's dissolution on March 14, 1939, the power to review constitutional compliance in Slovakia passed to a constitutional collegium composed of the Supreme and Supreme Administrative Court Senate chairpersons, which never adjudicated any cases.[11]

Post-World War II, the 1948 and 1960 Constitutions omitted any reference to a constitutional court, transferring the task of constitutional review to the National Assembly's leadership and eliminating external parliamentary oversight, which remained largely theoretical.[12]

Discussion of actual constitutional review resumes only after the 1989 changes. The Constitutional Court of the Czechoslovak Federation (CCFC) was formed in 1991, featuring 12 judges appointed for seven years by the

---

9 Law on the Constitutional Court no. 162/1920 Coll.

10 Alexander Bröstl, Pavel Holländer and Patrik Príbelský, *Ústavné Právo Slovenskej Republiky* (Vydavatelství a nakladatelství Aleš Čeněk 2021). See Law no. 147/1933 Coll. and law no. 109/1934. Coll.

11 Para 1 of law no. 20/1942 Coll.

12 See art 65, sub 1 of constitutional law no. 150/1948 Coll., and art 41, sub 2 in constitutional law no. 100/1960 Coll. See also art 36, sub 4 of constitutional law no. 143/1968.

president and elected by the Federal Assembly and the Czech and Slovak National Assemblies, ensuring an equal number of Czech and Slovak judges.[13] During its brief tenure, the CCFC influenced the development of democratic institutions in Czechoslovakia, delivering five plenary decisions and declaring three statutes unconstitutional.

The introduction of constitutional law no. 460/1992 Coll. officially established the SCC. While it aspired to continue the constitutional court's tradition from the 1920s, its design was more strongly inspired by the centralized constitutional powers in the 1963 Yugoslavian constitution.[14]

Following the 1989 transition to democracy and a market economy, the CCFC and the SCC played crucial roles in shaping the constitutional framework. They were pivotal in ensuring legal certainty and establishing stable political and economic standards. Despite the limited number of decisions during its brief tenure, the CCFC's early judgments were foundational for the emerging constitutional order. These initial rulings were particularly significant as the Court aimed to address the nation's authoritarian past.

There were crucial matters of the emerging rule of law that needed to be settled. First, lustration, or the vetting process typical of transitioning democracies, became a focal point. This process often led public officials to leave office, either in pursuit of private sector rewards or due to the threat of being subjected to lustration. Intended to block former communist state security collaborators, Communist Party leaders, and graduates of Soviet ideological schools from entering government and other key sectors, lustration laws sparked controversy across Central and Eastern Europe. Constitutional courts frequently evaluated their legality, leading to varying interpretations.[15]

Furthermore, issues like restitution of property ownership,[16] penal sanctions,[17] and retroactivity of the legal norms needed to be resolved.[18] Moreover,

---

13 See constitutional law no. 91/1991 Coll. and law no. 491/1991 Coll.

14 Ján Štiavnický and Max Steuer, 'The Constitutional Court of the Slovak Republic: The Many Faces of Law-Making by a Constitutional Court with Extensive Review Powers' in Monika Florczak-Wątor (ed), Judicial Law-Making in European Constitutional Courts (Routledge 2020) 184.

15 Compare for instance the decision of the CCC PL ÚS 1/92 from 26 November 1992 and the Hungarian Alkotmánybíróság (AB) [Constitutional Court] no. 11/1992.

16 Decision of the SCC PL ÚS 597/92.

17 Decision of the SCC PL ÚS 13/93.

18 Decision of the SCC PL ÚS. 78/92, PL ÚS 36/95.

SCC set the limits of individual rights,[19] roles of constitutional authorities, fundamental principles of separation of power,[20] independence of the judiciary, and the right to a lawful judge,[21] or a distinction between the president's action as a representative of the state and an individual.[22]

Overall, the SCC played an integral role in addressing new challenges within the legal culture, interpreting hierarchical public administration relations, and defining federal and state powers post-Velvet Revolution. Its progressive decisions have profoundly impacted the safeguarding and evolution of democratic governance and judicial independence in Slovakia.

The strong position of the SCC was justified by the undisputed claim that it does not review the state of affairs but the infringement of rights.[23]

3.4 SCC losing breath

Although there was an initial period when the SCC was trying to set its own space in the system of the Slovak Republic, when the revolutionary enthusiasm was gone, it became apparent that the SCC was stuck to be a tool for furthering either judicial or political interest.

Most influential decisions showcased an uneasy mix of adherence to the rule of law principles and the impact of judicial collegiality or political pressures. This heightened pressure is understandable due to the Court's powerful role and the political ambition surrounding judicial appointments. This dynamic is illustrated by analyzing several noteworthy decisions that caught international attention.

3.5 The existence of the Special Court[24]

In response to extensive criminal activity and corruption during the 1990s, the National Council established a new Special Court (SC) in 2003.[25] Due to

---

19 Decision of the SCC PL ÚS 5/92.
20 Decision of the SCC PL ÚS 16/95.
21 Decision of the SCC I ÚS 8/94.
22 Decision of the SCC II ÚS. 312/92.
23 Decision of the SCC I ÚS 205/92.
24 Decision of the SCC PL ÚS 17/08.
25 The law on the Special Court no. 458/2003 Coll.

the special qualifications required and the risks associated with handling corruption cases, this court was integrated into the judicial system with markedly higher salaries for its judges. These increased salaries contributed to the legal challenge against the SC, alongside claims that the SC functioned as an extraordinary court with jurisdiction focused on representatives of state authorities and its judges' security clearances subject to National Security Authority (NSA) review.[26]

The SCC raised several concerns. The laws governing the SC and the protection of confidential information allowed the NSA to collect sensitive data on SC judges and their relatives, compromising standards of judicial independence.[27] Further, judicial appointments required NSA approval, thus giving excessive power to the executive. By a narrow majority of one vote, the SCC sided with a group of MPs contesting the SC.

The SCC did not perform a standard proportionality test, claiming the pay disparity was unjustified. Following the May 2009 verdict, general court judges began filing anti-discrimination claims, citing the Anti-discrimination Act, and calculating potential earnings had they been SC judges, claiming non-pecuniary damages. Nearly two-thirds of Slovak judges took legal action against the Slovak Republic.

Six dissenting judges of the SCC criticized what they saw as undue judicial activism by the majority. The controversy deepened when the National Council replaced the SC with the Specialized Criminal Court, bestowing nearly identical competencies and keeping the same personnel, apart from adjusting salaries.[28] The fallout included almost a thousand anti-discrimination claims seeking millions in damages and several SC cases needing reopening due to the SC's unconstitutionality.

Despite ruling the SC unconstitutional, the SCC specified that this decision did not affect the status of individuals already convicted, effectively acting

---

[26] See in James E Moliterno, Lucia Berdisová, Peter Čuroš, and Ján Mazúr, 'Independence without Accountability: The Harmful Consequences of EU Policy toward Central and Eastern European Entrants' (2018) 42 Fordham Int'l LJ 481.

[27] Tomáš Ľalík, 'The Slovak Constitutional Court on Unconstitutional Constitutional Amendment (Pl. ÚS 21/2014)' (2020) 16 *European Constitutional Law Review* 328, 333.

[28] Ladislav Orosz, *Ústavný Súd Slovenskej Republiky v III. Funkčnom Období-Hodnotenie Zainteresovaného* (o Sebareflexii a Užitočných Odkazoch Pre Nasledovníkov 2019) 78. See the law on the Specialized Criminal Court no. 291/2009 Coll.

as a legislative decision that thwarted any hope for them to have their cases reheard in criminal courts. This highlights that the Special Court issue was not centered on individual rights but on the broader structural design of the Slovak judiciary system.[29]

3.6 The appointment of the prosecutor general[30]

In 2012, the SCC addressed a dispute concerning whether the president of the country was obligated to follow the National Council's recommendation for appointing the prosecutor general.[31] On June 17, 2011, the National Council elected a candidate, but President Ivan Gašparovič delayed the appointment while awaiting the SCC decision regarding amendments to the prosecutor general's election process.[32] The SCC later determined that the public vote by parliament members adhered to the constitution, yet the president still declined to appoint the selected candidate.[33]

Those challenging the president's decision argued that he was obstructing constitutional processes, preventing effective institutional functioning. Conversely, the president defended his actions, citing concerns that the candidate may not have met the necessary moral requirements. The SCC intervened, assuming the role of clarifying constitutional ambiguities not explicitly addressed by the constitution. Their decision effectively empowered the president, stating he is obligated under Article 102 of the Constitution to act on the National Council's proposal unless the candidate fails to meet moral criteria or possesses personal factors affecting their ability to uphold office duties. The president must provide clear reasons for non-appointments to ensure actions aren't arbitrary.

The controversy deepened when, in another decision, the SCC found that the rights of Jozef Čentéš, the candidate elected by the National Council, had been violated when President Gašparovič refused his appointment, instead

---

29 Štiavnický and Steuer (n 13) 190.

30 Decision of the SCC PL ÚS 4/2012.

31 Decision of the SCC PL ÚS 4/2012.

32 Previous elections were done by secret vote; the change enacted shortly before the election turned the vote into public vote.

33 Decision of the SCC PL ÚS 95/2011.

swearing in another candidate.[34] By that time, the new candidate, Jaromír Čižnár, had already assumed the role of prosecutor general.

In 2015, a similar case concerning the president's obligation to appoint SCC justices took a surprising turn.[35] While many expected a ruling consistent with the previous decision concerning the prosecutor general, the SCC ruled differently and was influenced by significant political changes. By then, SMER-SD, previously in opposition, held a majority, and President Andrej Kiska was at odds with P. M. Robert Fico, whose party controlled a large portion of the National Council. The SCC, however, retained its composition.

President Kiska received six candidates from which he was to select three for vacant SCC positions. He appointed only one and sought additional nominations for the remaining seats. The National Council chairman refused, asserting that parliament had fulfilled its responsibilities. Subsequently, three rejected candidates claimed their rights were violated, and the SCC sided with them, reinstating their candidacy.[36] The SCC argued that the constitution required the president to select from the proposed candidates without further scrutiny. Ultimately, the dispute was resolved when another seat became vacant, allowing for a compromise with new and existing candidate appointments.

The SCC ruled that the president is constitutionally obliged to select one of the two proposed candidates for the SCC vacancy, negating the need for further evaluation, which is opposite to what the SCC rendered in the decision on the prosecutor general.

3.7 The Mečiar amnesties case[37]

In a significant transitional justice ruling, the SCC approved nullifying the amnesties granted by Prime Minister Vladimír Mečiar, who was exercising presidential powers to block potential investigations into alleged state secret

---

[34] Decision of the SCC I ÚS 397/2014.

[35] Decision of the SCC PL ÚS 45/2015.

[36] Lívia Trellová and Boris Balog, 'Misconceived Quest for the Perfect Constitutional Court' (2020) 16 *Balkan Soc Sci Rev* 107, 113.

[37] Decision of the SCC PL ÚS 7/2017.

service crimes involving him.[38] Before 2017, the SCC lacked the authority to review these amnesties, which only became possible after a constitutional amendment empowered it to do so.[39] Notably, the SCC was tasked with assessing the constitutionality of the National Council's annulment of the amnesty rather than the initial amnesty decisions themselves.

In reaching its decision, the SCC considered the European Court of Human Rights' conservative stance on amnesty and pardon, which does allow constitutional review of amnesty decisions. International legal standards recognize two main criteria for annulment: the seriousness of the act and the beneficiary's identity, particularly in cases of self-amnesty by state officials—conditions met by the Slovak case.

The case centered on two decisions made by Mečiar, then acting as interim president: one on March 3, 1998,[40] and another on July 7, 1998.[41] The first decision involved a "failed referendum," where the minister of the interior issued ballots missing a question, against the president's and SCC's directive. The SCC determined that granting amnesty for this violated constitutional human rights. The second amnesty involved the 1995 abduction of Michal Kováč Jr., son of then-President Michal Kováč, to Austria.[42] Evidence suggested it was an operation led by the Slovak secret service, implicating Mečiar in misusing government power against a political adversary.

Mečiar publicly defended his actions, claiming the amnesties were necessary for social stability. However, the SCC viewed them as exacerbating social tensions by conflicting with the principles of the rule of law. The ruling highlighted a tussle between ensuring legal certainty for those granted amnesty and maintaining broader legal integrity for the nation.

---

[38] Decision of the SCC PL ÚS 7/2017.

[39] Constitutional law no. 71/2017 Coll.

[40] Published under decision of the prime minister no. 55/1998 Coll.

[41] Published under decision of the prime minister no. 214/1998 Coll.

[42] The minister of the interior did not change his decision even though the SCC decided on the incompetence of the government in meddling with the referendum questions. See decisions II.ÚS 30/97 and II.ÚS 31/97. Michál Ovádek, '"*Unrichtiges Recht" in Slovakia? The Radbruch Formula and Positive Law from the Nineties*' (*VerfBlog*, 2017/2/07) <https://verfassungsblog.de/unrichtiges-recht-in-slovakia-the-radbruch-formula-and-positive-law-from-the-nineties/> accessed 20 November 2024.

Ultimately, the SCC concluded that preserving legal certainty for individuals suspected of grave offenses could not outweigh the foundational constitutional principles. The annulment did not infringe upon the presumption of innocence or the right to a fair trial guaranteed by the constitution and international human rights treaties. The SCC upheld the National Council's annulment of Mečiar's amnesty decisions from March 3, 1998, and July 7, 1998.[43] Dissenting opinions from Justices Brňák and Ľalík emphasized a formalist perspective, arguing that the absence of legal barriers should have rendered the amnesties valid.[44]

3.8 The "substantial core of the constitution" case[45]

Slovakia's constitution is among Europe's most amendable, requiring only a three-fifths parliamentary majority to adopt a constitutional act. This has sparked debate among constitutional lawyers about whether the constitution should have an unamenable core.[46]

Since the 1989 transition from state socialism, constitutional courts have operated on the premise that the National Council refrains from amending the "substantial core" of the constitution, and the MPs have not challenged

---

43 Decision of the National Assembly no. 570 of 5 April 2017.

44 Ján Mazák and Ladislav Orosz, 'Quashing the Decisions on Amnesty in the Constitutional System of the Slovak Republic: Opening or Closing Pandora's Box?' (2018) 8 *The Lawyer Quarterly* 2.

45 Pl. ÚS 21/2014, from 30.1.2019. For a detailed analysis, see Marek Domin *'A Part of the Constitution Is Unconstitutional, the Slovak Constitutional Court Has Ruled'* (*VerfBlog*, 8 February 2019) <https://verfassungsblog.de/a-part-of-the-constitution-is-unconstitutional-the-slovak-constitutional-court-has-ruled/> accessed 20 November 2024.

46 See Marta Breichová Lapčáková, *Ústava a Ústavné Zákony* (Kalligram 2013); Boris Balog, *Materiálne Jadro Ústavy Slovenskej Republiky* (Eurokódex 2014); Ladislav Orosz, 'K Problémom Kompatibility Ústavného Systému Slovenskej Republiky' (2005) 57 *Justičná revue*; Ondřej Preuss, 'Demokratický Právní Stát Tesaný Do Pískovce' (2016) 24 *Časopis pro právní vědu a praxi*; Maxim Tomoszek, 'Nezměnitelnost Materiálního Jádra Ústavy Jako Řešení Konfliktu Ústavních Hodnot' (2010) 18 *Časopis pro právní vědu a praxi*.

the compliance of constitutional acts with the constitution itself.[47] This approach persisted until 2014, when Amendment of the Constitution no. 161/2014 Coll. was enacted, introducing vetting procedures for new judges and control mechanisms for sitting judges. Legislators recognized the need to address judicial integrity concerns and considered Slovakia's evolving socio-political landscape. According to the explanatory report, the amendment sought to enhance judicial efficacy by limiting judges' immunity—allowing them to retain only functional immunity—and eliminating the need for SCC consent for judicial prosecution.[48] Additionally, the amendment expanded the Judicial Council's authority and separated its chair from the chief justice position.[49]

Amendment 161/2014's most debated element was its transitional provision regarding judicial competence, which stipulated that judges appointed before July 1, 2014, could be dismissed if they failed to meet competence standards.[50] These standards, intended to ensure judicial function, were to be assessed by the Judicial Council based on National Security Authority (NSA) reports, encompassing details of personal and professional backgrounds.[51]

The chairwoman of the Judicial Council challenged the application of these provisions, leading the SCC to suspend them in decision no. PL ÚS 21/2014. The Court noted that the Slovak constitution does not expressly address the unamendability of its articles as explicitly as some other constitutions do.[52] Without explicit constitutional provisions for immutability,

---

47 Simon Drugda, *Slovak Constitutional Court Strikes down a Constitutional Amendment – But the Amendment Remains Valid* (I-CONnectblog 2019) <http://www.iconnectblog.com/2019/04/slovak-constitutional-court-strikes-down-a-constitutional-amendment-but-the-amendment-remains-valid/> accessed 20 November 2024

48 It was a precondition; the judge could have been convicted only with the consent of the Constitutional Court.

49 As before the amendment, the chair of the Judicial Council and the president of the Supreme Court was connected.

50 Art. 154d, par. 3. of the Slovak Constitution.

51 Ibid. art. 154d, par. 1. See Ľalík, T Tracing Constitutional Changes in Slovakia between 2008–2016' (2017) 58 Hungarian Journal of Legal Studies 117.

52 For example: German Basic Law, art. 79 (3), Constitution of Norway, article 121, Constitution of Portugal, art. 288. Two fundamental decisions of the previous years appeared in the argumentation. Firstly, the decision of the SCC Pl. ÚS 7/2017 (Mečiar amnesties), and the decision of the SCC Pl. ÚS 17/08 (Special Court).

the concept of the constitution's "material core" remains implicit and shaped by SCC jurisprudence.[53] The Court asserted that judicial independence is essential to the rule of law.[54]

The decision PL ÚS 21/2014 was controversial as it delved deeper into substantive compliance of constitutional acts with the constitution than other European constitutional courts.[55] The decision's timing was also contentious, coinciding with the end of the Court's term when most justices were transitioning back to the Supreme Court. Suspicion arose that the president of the SCC might have sought to curry favor with the judiciary, possibly to bolster prospects for a forthcoming bid to become president of the Supreme Court. As a reaction to PL US 21/2014, the National Council amended the constitution, writing down explicitly that the SCC is not competent to review the compliance of constitutional acts with each other or the constitution. The lengthy discussion on the duty of the SCC to protect the "material core" that has not been mentioned in the constitution explicitly has been divided among those who support the "power of the sovereign" and those who support the SCC as "a guardian of the rule of law." After the constitutional amendment, the answer is clear. Even if there is "the material core," there is no authority to enforce it.

3.9 Decision on the amendment of the penal code[56]

After the Fico IV administration emerged in October 2023, it employed four key strategies to undermine democratic values and the rule of law in Slovakia. This period has starkly revealed the vulnerability of the Slovak legal system in the face of populist challenges. There were four pathways through which Slovakia experienced democratic backsliding. First, interference with the independence

[53] Principle of the rule of law in art. 1 par. 1 of the Slovak Constitution.

[54] Decision of the SCC PL ÚS 21/2014, par. 116.

[55] Austrian Constitutional Court in VfGH. 16.327/2001 from 11.11.2001, Ukrainian CC in decision no. 1-45/2010 from 30.9. 2010, Hungarian CC in decision no. 45/2012 AB from 28.12.2012 or Czech CC in decision no. Pl. ÚS 27/09 z 10.9.2009.

[56] decision of the SCC PL ÚS 3/2024.

of the judiciary,[57] deterioration of the democratic legislation process,[58] disqualification of associating toward common interest—attacks on civil society organizations,[59] and exerting political control over independent institutions.

There was an extensive amendment to the Penal Code in February 2024.[60] The Slovak government created general amnesty through the novelization of the Penal Code. It was adopted without consultations with experts and the public in a fast-track procedure. It affected all of the criminal offenses in the code, reduced penalties for corruption and criminal offenses against public safety and the environment, shortened statutes of limitations for all the crimes (including offenses against life, limb, or dignity), changed the position of cooperating defendants, strengthened the protection of judges against the criminal investigation and raised thresholds of damage by more than seven times what affected consideration between a criminal offense and a misdemeanor. In March 2024, the SCC postponed the effectivity of the amendment.[61] This step heightened the expectations of both legal and lay communities since the effect of the amended Penal Code would mean a general pardon on many criminal offenses already committed, investigated, and prosecuted. The reason was that under existing legal practice, someone charged with a criminal offense was subject to the most

---

57 PM Fico verbally intimidated the Slovak Constitutional Court after the plenum of 12 judges decided to suspend the Penal Code and Criminal Procedure Code amendments. Furthermore, verbal intimidation targeted ordinary courts, Specialized Criminal Court and Supreme Court judges, the Minister of Justice instructed to inspect the Supreme Court and the Specialized Criminal Court to examine the random allocation of individual cases interference with the Council for the Judiciary. Since the parliamentary election in September 2023, half of the members of the Judicial Council have been dismissed, and seven of them have been replaced, now including the representatives appointed by the President of the country. Nine council members have changed in the past nine months.

58 The fourth government of Robert Fico has passed nearly 60% of laws through fast-track legislative proceedings with no apparent justification in first 10 months of its tenure.

59 Moreover, the parliament approved the draft law on foreign influence and sent it to the second reading. Furthermore, the dialogue between the government and the third sector has been shut.

60 Draft law of amendment of the Penal Code 300/2005 Coll. See https://www.nrsr.sk/web/Dynamic/DocumentPreview.aspx?DocID=536597

61 Peter Čuroš, 'The Ides of March in Slovakia' (IACL-IADC blog, 23 April 2024) <https://blog-iacl-aidc.org/2024-posts/2024/4/23/the-ides-of-march-in-slovakia> accessed 20 November 2024

lenient conditions that applied during period their case was investigated or prosecuted.

At the beginning of summer 2024, both legal and lay communities in Slovakia were awaiting the SCC decision on the controversial penal legislation adopted in February 2024. The final decision, however, was everything, but not what was expected. The reasoning behind the SCC's decision in the PL ÚS 3/2024 case will serve as a stark reminder of a missed opportunity for years, if not decades. At a time when the unchecked rise of populist governments threatened the very fabric of democratic society, the SCC chose to turn a blind eye and a deaf ear, missing a crucial chance to avert this dangerous trend.

The SCC resolved undoubtedly one of the most complex and important decisions since the establishment of the Slovak Republic within 134 days from the first proposal submitted by the President of the Slovak Republic. The gravity of this decision, comparable to the decision under the popular title "material core of the constitution" (PL ÚS 21/2014), which took nearly four and a half years, should not be underestimated. The short period necessarily affected the soundness and persuasiveness of the arguments used by the SCC.

The refusal to set boundaries for the legislative power in violating the rules of the legislative process was a missed opporunity. The SCC acknowledged that none of the declared facts for which the parliamentary majority wanted to adopt an amendment to the penal laws in a fast-track legislative procedure were legitimate. Neither the incorrect implementation of directives of the European Parliament and Council, nor the decision of the Constitutional Court PL ÚS 1/2021, nor the need to respond to inflation, nor the alignment of regulations with decisions of the ECtHR in individual cases, nor the conflict between the General Prosecutor's Office and the Special Prosecutor's Office were reasons for the fast-track legislative proceedings according to the SCC. The majority breached the law on the Rules of Procedure of the National Council of the Slovak Republic, Act No. 350/1996 Coll.[62]

The SCC, surprisingly, concluded it did not matter that the law had been breached. The only thing that mattered was that the parliamentary minority could say something. However, it did not matter that nobody listened to them,

62 Act on the rules of procedure the National Council of the Slovak Republic no. 350/1996 Coll.

that the proposers of the bill did not respond to them because they were not present, nor that the majority forced them to use the precious limited debate time in the middle of the night. And finally, it did not matter that a third of the proposal changed the day before the vote.[63] According to the SCC, all of this was a matter of political strategy. Despite many references to the decisions of the Czech Constitutional Court, the SCC hasn't addressed the fact that its counterpart was willing to examine unconstitutionality in adopting a legal norm.[64]

In the fifth part of the decision, we enter the dark waters of constitutional argumentation. Here, a didactic lecture begins on what deserves and does not deserve to be an argument from the proposers[65] or about how the proposers dared to argue the purpose of punishment.[66] The SCC fully accepted the reasoning of the Ministry of Justice. For example, indicted MPs can propose laws to reduce the penalties they face and shorten the statute of limitations because the change will affect all defendants in such situations. From the decision, we also learn that the indicted MPs acted correctly when they voted in their favor because they would breach their duties as MPs if they abstained.

One is stunned as to why the SCC is doing such extra work. If the parliamentary opposition criticized the lack of arguments in the explanatory memorandum to the amendment of the criminal laws, the SCC diligently supplemented them in these points.

3.10 Conclusion

While the original intention was to create a Kelsenian constitutional court that would fulfill the tasks of the guardian of the constitution, what developed from the initial idea was, in fact, a political tool for furthering the interests of judges and politicians. Despite copying the solutions from the "center," the Slovak constitutional judiciary has not developed into an independent institution. This was visible in the selection process, which has always been in the center of the political attention. The weak position of the constitutional court is visible in its

63 Draft law of amendment of the Penal Code 300/2005 Coll.
64 See decision of the SCC PL ÚS 27/09.
65 Decision of the SCC PL ÚS 3/2024, para 306.
66 Decision of the SCC PL ÚS 3/2024, para 366.

crucial decisions. In the decision on the SC, it was no secret that various interests were competing. On the one hand, the political interest of the government was strong in the fight against corruption; on the other, it was the judicial interest supported by the parliamentary opposition at the time. In the end, the judicial interest prevailed, entitling all judges in Slovakia to require compensation for discriminatory treatment. The only outcome of the dissolution of the Special Court was chaos and damages that judges sought from the state.

In the second case of the appointment of the prosecutor general, it was possible to observe the political interest of President Gašparovič, strongly supported by the parliamentary opposition led by the party SMER-SD, who did not allow the elected candidate to be appointed. Despite the court's conclusion that the rights of the elected candidate Jozef Čentéš were infringed, he never became prosecutor general. The strong position of the prosecutor general and the latent interests behind the scenes were the primary reasons why the anti-corruption administration led by Iveta Radičová did not survive and lost their majority after only 15 months.

In the third case of an appointment of the judges at the SCC, it was again possible to observe competing interests between, at the time, ruling SMER-SD and President Kiska. Once again, the SMER-SD interest has prevailed through obscure distinguishing from the situation in the case of the prosecutor general.

While the decision on the annulment of amnesties awarded by Vladimír Mečiar seems to portray a strong constitutional court, the constitutional court's role was quite passive. Although the court analyzed whether the decision of the parliament to annul the amnesty awarded in the past, the main question was the one that was answered three years later—is it within the power of the constitutional court to contradict the power of the National Council prescribed by the constitution?

We found the answer to this question in the decision on the material core of the constitution. Here, the constitutional court embraced itself to shut down the sovereign's decision and was strongly punished for it soon after, when the National Council explicitly adopted that the SCC has no power to decide on the compliance of various parts of the constitution. In this decision, which was the last decision of the term of the court, the SCC furthered the judicial interest. The controversy of this decision contributed to the fact that within the legal community, the decision was perceived as a gift to the judicial colleagues before many justices returned to their original courts.

The decision on the Penal Code amendment is the most controversial among all the mentioned decisions. In this decision, the constitutional court entirely subordinated to the political interest by abdicating the guardianship of the constitution and giving the legislator full power over the content and the process of adopting laws.

In conclusion, despite high hopes of being "Hüter der Verfassung," the SCC has never really settled into this position. In its decision-making, observing the competition of interests instead of a stable doctrine has been a constant possibility.

Bibliography

Balog B., *Materiálne Jadro Ústavy Slovenskej Republiky* (Eurokódex 2014).

Breichová Lapčáková M., *Ústava a Ústavné Zákony* (Kalligram 2013).

Bröstl A., Holländer P. and Príbelský P., *Ústavné Právo Slovenskej Republiky. Vydavatelství a nakladatelství* (Aleš Čeněk, 2021).

Čuroš P., The Ides of March in Slovakia, IACL-IADC blog, <https://blog-iacl-aidc.org/2024-posts/2024/4/23/the-ides-of-march-in-slovakia>.

Domin M., "A Part of the Constitution Is Unconstitutional, the Slovak Constitutional Court Has Ruled" *(VerfBlog*, February 8, 2019) <https://verfassungsblog.de/a-part-of-the-constitution-is-unconstitutional-the-slovak-constitutional-court-has-ruled/> accessed November 20, 2024.

Drugda S., Slovak Constitutional Court Strikes down a Constitutional Amendment—But the Amendment Remains Valid (I-CONnectblog 2019) <http://www.iconnectblog.com/2019/04/slovak-constitutional-court-strikes-down-a-constitutional-amendment-but-the-amendment-remains-valid/> accessed November 20, 2024.

Harmathy A., "Codification in a Period of Transition" (1998) 31 *U.C. Davis Law Review* 783.

Kühn Z., *The Judiciary in Central and Eastern Europe: Mechanical Jurisprudence in Transformation?* (Martinus Nijhoff Publishers 2011).

Ľalík T., "Tracing Constitutional Changes in Slovakia between 2008–2016" (2017) 58 *Hungarian Journal of Legal Studies* 117.

Ľalík T., "The Slovak Constitutional Court on Unconstitutional Constitutional Amendment (PL ÚS 21/2014)" (2020) 16 *European Constitutional Law Review* 328.

Mazák J. and Orosz L., "Quashing the Decisions on Amnesty in the Constitutional System of the Slovak Republic: Opening or Closing Pandora's Box?" (2018) 8 *The Lawyer Quarterly.*

Moliterno J. E., Berdisová L., Čuroš P. and Mazúr J., "Independence without Accountability: The Harmful Consequences of EU Policy toward Central and Eastern European Entrants" (2018) 42 *Fordham Int'l LJ* 481.

Orosz L., "K Problémom Kompatibility Ústavného Systému Slovenskej Republiky" (2005) 57 *Justičná revue.*

Orosz L., "Ústavný Súd Slovenskej Republiky v III. Funkčnom Období-Hodnotenie Zainteresovaného (o Sebareflexii a Užitočných Odkazoch Pre Nasledovníkov)" (2019) *Ústavné Dni* 68.

Ovádek M., "'Unrichtiges Recht' in Slovakia? The Radbruch Formula and Positive Law from the Nineties" *(VerfBlog,* February 7, 2017) <https://verfassungsblog.de/unrichtiges-recht-in-slovakia-the-radbruch-formula-and-positive-law-from-the-nineties/> accessed November 20, 2024.

Preuss O., "Demokratický Právní Stát Tesaný Do Pískovce" (2016) 24 *Časopis pro právní vědu a praxi* 365

Schmitt C., *The Concept of the Political* (tr Schwab G, University of Chicago Press 1996).

Štiavnický J. and Steuer M., "The Constitutional Court of the Slovak Republic: The Many Faces of Law-Making by a Constitutional Court with Extensive Review Powers' in Monika Florczak-Wątor (ed.), *Judicial Law-Making in European Constitutional Courts* (Routledge 2020).

Tomoszek M., "Nezměnitelnost Materiálního Jádra Ústavy Jako Řešení Konfliktu Ústavních Hodnot" (2010) 18 *Časopis pro právní vědu a praxi* 325.

Trellová L. and Balog B., "Misconceived Quest for the Perfect Constitutional Court" (2020) 16 *Balkan Soc Sci Rev* 107.

Vinx L., *The Guardian of the Constitution: Hans Kelsen and Carl Schmitt on the Limits of Constitutional Law* (Cambridge University Press 2015)

Dynamic Concepts of Constitutional Identity Through the Lens of Hume, Hobbes, and Selected Psychological Approaches

Adam Demczuk

ABSTRACT
This chapter investigates the multifaceted concept of constitutional identity (CI), examining both its static and dynamic dimensions, and their intersection with personal and group identity theories. The study underscores the significance of aligning CI with principles from the social sciences to gain a more comprehensive understanding of this intricate concept. The research analyzes two primary approaches to CI: the static sense, grounded in the Weimar tradition, and the dynamic sense, which places a significant emphasis on the constitutional subject. The research advocates for a clear demarcation between static and dynamic approaches to CI, aiming to enhance the focus and validity of research in this field. Additionally, the study encourages the utilization of empirical qualitative research methods to further deepen our comprehension of dynamic CI.

Keywords: Constitutional identity, static and dynamic understandings of identity, empirical research of constitutional identity

4.1 Introduction to dynamic and static concepts of constitutional identity

Undefined boundaries of the concept of constitutional identity (CI) allow for seeking its semantics in various research areas. For an inherently vague term, it is crucial to determine how constitutional identity can draw from the definition of identity itself. Identity as such is a concept rooted in the social sciences; therefore, it is worth considering to what extent the understanding of constitutional identity corresponds to the interests of the social sciences in human identity. It will be important here to examine the possibility of interpreting constitutional identity in the same way as one interprets the identity of an individual or a group of individuals and how scientific considerations related to the concept of CI can benefit from such interpretation.

Michał Ziółkowski proposed two approaches to the term of CI—static and dynamic sense.[1] The static sense derives from the so-called Weimar tradition

---

[1] Michał Ziółkowski, "Dwie Płaszczyzny Dyskusji o Tożsamości Konstytucyjnej (Teoria *versus* Dogmatyka) in Andrzej Wróbel and Michał Ziółkowski (eds), *Tożsamość Konstytucyjna w Wybranych Państwach Członkowskich Unii Europejskiej* (Wolters Kluwer 2021).

and involves finding unchanging norms, morally significant values, or stable institutions characterizing a particular constitution. This understanding is called static mainly because the reflection dedicated to it does not take into account changes over time in the constitutional subject, and the aforementioned elements contributing to it are stable and relatively unchanging. The dynamic sense, on the other hand, assumes the shaping of the constitutional subject in a discursive manner. In this approach, identity not only includes elements directly derived from the written constitution but also encompasses historical and social experiences. This approach is currently employed by most theoretical models of identity, such as those proposed by Gary J. Jacobsohn, Michel Rosenfeld, or Anna Śledzińska-Simon.[2]

On the one hand, identity can be understood as sameness. This comprehension of identity in some way can correspond to the static understanding of CI. Components of such CI are, for example, unamendable norms, institutions, traditions—or in the case of Poland—boundaries of conferral of competencies.[3] When we approach the topic through the mentioned aspects, we can refer to classical theories of CI, both appearing in jurisprudence or earlier, positivist legal theory. Static theories offer simplified and concrete explanations of what can be changed within the constitutional system. However, the field in which those theories don't offer explanations is historicity, mechanisms of change, and legitimization of power.

Dynamic concepts of CI are in some way an answer to the issue, emphasizing the constitutional subject. This subject can be understood as the constitutional core that strides through history and is an emanation of the sovereign. Three main dynamic theories approach the notion of constitutional

---

2 Gary Jeffrey Jacobsohn, *Constitutional Identity* (Harvard University Press 2010); Michel Rosenfeld, *The Identity of the Constitutional Subject. Selfhood, Citizenship, Culture and Community* (Routledge 2010); Anna Śledzińska-Simon, Koncepcja Tożsamości Konstytucyjnej: Wymiar Indywidualny, Relatywny oraz Zbiorowy (2016) Acta Universitatis Wratislaviensis 335; In this work, I will refer to Polish paper of Śledzińska-Simon because Polish is her native language. However, almost identical concept is presented in English paper: Anna Śledzińska-Simon, "Constitutional identity in 3D: A model of individual, relational, and collective self and its application in Poland" (2015) 13 *International Journal of Constitutional Law* 124.

3 Anna Śledzińska-Simon and Michał Ziółkowski, *Constitutional Identity of Poland: Is the Emperor Putting on the Old Clothes of Sovereignty?* (2017) <https://dx.doi.org/10.2139/ssrn.2997407>.

subject differently. However, all assign it to the imagined community[4] or the world of ideas.[5]

First, we have Jacobsohn's concept of CI. In his theory, the CI is constructed based on national experiences.[6] However, what Jacobsohn underlines is that this identity is neither any absolutely objective nor subjective matter. Neither this identity is internally coherent. It "emerges dialogically"[7] as a representation of a "mix of political aspirations and commitments that are expressive of a nation's past, as well as the determination of those within the society who seek in some ways to transcend that past."[8] Therefore, the subject of CI is a social and collective actor with multiple values from which, through experiences within dialectical and historical processes constructs a sense of self.

Second, the constitutional subject plays a main role in the theory proposed by Rosenfeld.[9] However, the subject is not simply an imagined community.[10] His theory of CI is based on a constitutional subject understood as the sovereign (e.g., "We, the People"). However, this subject exists as an abstract entity in some way. The structure of the subject is in no way coherent. The "self" of the constitutional subject on many levels is incoherent with other selves. However, on the final level, the subject can be imagined as coherent as a single self.[11] Despite being constructed, reconstructed, and reevaluated, the emergent unified identity possesses qualities such as one (never complete) sameness, self, and selfhood (or personality).[12] The subject must be also considered as a "lack" in Lacanian and Freudian understanding of the word.[13] The whole drive for the emergence of the constitutional subject is the lack of legitimacy and authority

4 Ziółkowski (n 1) 308.

5 Adam Demczuk, "Tożsamość Człowieka jako Punkt Wyjścia dla Rozumienia Tożsamości Konstytucyjnej. Wybrane Koncepcje Filozoficzne i Psychologiczne" in Monika Florczak Wątor and Marcin Krzemiński (eds), *Interdyscyplinarny Wymiar Tożsamości Konstytucyjnej*.

6 Gary Jeffrey Jacobsohn, *Constitutional Identity* (Harvard University Press 2010), 7.

7 ibid.: However, one may wonder whether the word term *dialectically* would be more accurate.

8 ibid.

9 Rosenfeld (n 2) 26.

10 Ziółkowski (n 1) 308.

11 ibid. 41.

12 ibid. 23–4.

13 ibid. 36.

for the constitutional order.[14] This would explain why the subject is in constant need of constructing the self—it was deprived of the Great Other at the bottom of the Unconscious, which would legitimize the current constitutional order and every law within the state that emerges from this order. However, as the constitution is the final law, that emanates with its meaning to the whole legal system, the constitutional subject as a unified abstract being, cannot adhere to the norms created by the Great Other, because it doest have anyone to put in its place. Therefore, the constitutional subject can be thought of as a psychotic structure of the Unconscious that is in need of creating the Great Other because of the lack of the final legitimization within this abstract entity.[15] Unfortunately, Rosenfeld did not refer to the structure of the Unconscious with obvious psychotic attributes. It is more unclear why Rosenfeld has resorted to explaining the dialectical processes within the subject in terms of neurotic defense mechanisms such as negation, metaphor, or metonymy.[16]

Third, also relevant to the topic of personal identity as a means to understand the CI is the theory proposed by Śledzińska-Simon. The author argues that every identity that emerged through the constitution and its historicity is composed of constitutional dimensions of self, which are individual, relative, and collective. The author argues that this tripartition is accurate because Freud used also a tripartite concept of the psyche.[17] This argument is somewhat not accurate, however, the three dimensions are useful tools for the constitutional subject to address itself, its relations, and its place in the collective international community.[18] The individual dimension in which the subject refers to the self through history, individuality, culture, etc. is used to determine the immanent cultural, national, and legal institutions for constitutional order and CI.[19] The relative dimension describes how the constitutional self refers to other constitutional subjects, such as different

14 ibid.

15 Sigmund Freud, *The Loss of Reality* (first published 1924); Rosenfeld doesn't explain it in the terms of the psychotic structure, yet I think it is more adequate and proves better understanding of the subject he spokes of.

16 Rosenfeld (n 2) 65.

17 Anna Śledzińska-Simon, "Koncepcja Tożsamości Konstytucyjnej: Wymiar Indywidualny, Relatywny oraz Zbiorowy" (2016) Acta Universitatis Wratislaviensis 335.

18 ibid. 352.

19 ibid. 353.

states and intergovernmental organizations. Relative identity is created during interactions of the values in the international law.[20] The last dimension, collective, puts an emphasis on the identity of the subject as a part of supranational organization.[21] To demonstrate how this dimension is functioning, the best case study would be the European Union. The whole notion of CI "rose from the grave" as an answer to the question of the supremacy of EU law over the particular constitutional law of member states.[22] As the particular member states possess CI, the EU also has one.[23]

What is particularly visible, in all of the dynamic concepts there are references made to the subject as an analogy toward the human identity. Two main factors are visible in those theories. First—the identity of the subject resembles the personal identity described and explained in psychological and philosophical theories. Second—all of the three dynamic theories remain open for further use of personal identity theories. Jacobsohn claims that:

> There is a vast philosophical literature going back to Plato that continues to provide vibrant, and sometimes passionate, debate over the criteria for determining identity, at least on the personal level. Much of this controversy surrounding the status of personhood is not directly transferable to constitutional matters, although constitutional theorists would be wise to give it measured consideration as an aid in structuring how we might reflect on the subject of identity and constitutions, and why it should matter to those who theorize about constitutions.[24]

It seems that this theory opens a broader field of study for CI scholars. Hence, not only are philosophical ideas most welcome but are sometimes necessary to elaborate on the topic. Furthermore, philosophical ideas appear in Rosenfeld's interpretation of the notion:

> The conception of the identity of the constitutional subject as originating in a lack or absence bears strong affinities to certain philosophical and psychoanalytical theories of the subject.[25]

---

20 ibid. 353–4.
21 ibid. 354–5.
22 Federico Fabbrini and András Sajó, "The dangers of constitutional identity" (2018) 25 *European Law Journal* 457; Elke Cloots, "National Identity, Constitutional Identity, and Sovereignty in the EU" (2016) 45 *Netherlands Journal of Legal Philosophy* 82.
23 Śledzińska-Simon (n 17) 354–6.
24 Jacobsohn (n 2) 7.
25 Rosenfeld (n 2) 36.

In addition to philosophical reflection, especially one of Hegel, we can see the use of the psychoanalytical theories of Freud and Lacan. As mentioned earlier, psychoanalysis as an interpretation method of CI can explain the topic and provide unparalleled understanding. What follows such interpretations are references to the theories of unconsciousness and through that to psychology as a science about unconscious mechanisms governing the identity.[26] On the other hand, Śledzińska-Simon explicitly stated that "in social sciences, identity is most often analyzed as a cognitive element, motivational factor, and multifaceted entity."[27]

4.2 Constitutional Identity—Hume and Hobbes

Due to the openness of philosophical reflection, I propose to analyze CI by taking inspiration from two philosophers—namely David Hume and Thomas Hobbes. In both oeuvres we are able to find parallels of the state to person. The choice of the philosophers can be briefly explained—Hume compares the identity of a person to the identity of the state[28] and Hobbes compares the whole state to the person itself. Nonetheless, both understandings of identity will be elaborated in the following section.

4.2.1 Constitutional identity through the lens of Hume

According to Hume, identity isn't some ontological monistic being, neither a soul nor substance, not even an irreducible "self."[29] What is most interesting is that the last term is embraced by all dynamic theories of CI. Identity according to Hume is relational within any object of identity itself, ultimately created in the imagination of the human mind. Hume argues that the identity of a person or so-called self is nothing more than subsequent perceptions or other events that people attribute finality and wishful thinking to.[30]

---

[26] Andrea Zagaria, Agata Ando and Alessandro Zennaro, "Psychology: A Giant with Feet of Clay" (2020) 54 *Integrative Psychological and Behavioral Science* 521.

[27] Śledzińska-Simon (n 17), 351.

[28] David Hume, *Treatise of Human Nature* (first published 1739–40, Clarendon Press 1896).

[29] ibid. 251.

[30] ibid. 251.

The main relations between perceptions in the human mind, that allow us to acknowledge personal identity are resemblance, causation, and contiguity.[31] The central mediator between those three is memory. First of all, the resemblance is a relation between past and present events that allows us to perceive similar events as the same, due to the work of our memory as a "[…] faculty, by which we raise up images of past perceptions […]."[32] Causation refers to the human mind as a "system of different perceptions" that are in the causal chain of modifying each other.[33] Memory is also responsible for the contiguity of different perceptional events. We rely on it to place in time different events and on that basis, sensation of continuity and coherence emerges.[34]

To better explain the causality and continuity of events as identity, Hume applies the metaphor of the state:

> In this respect, I cannot compare the soul more properly to anything than. to a republic or commonwealth, in which the several members are united by the reciprocal ties of government and subordination, and give rise to other persons, who propagate the same republic in the incessant changes of its parts. And as the same individual, republic may not only change its members, but also its laws and constitutions; in like manner the same person may vary his character and disposition, as well as his impressions and ideas, without losing his identity.[35]

If the above were transferred to the notion of CI, the CI could be understood as being an illusion composed of the relations of resemblance, causality, and contiguity. Yet, the mentioned exercise of reduction could be achieved without losing the whole notion and impression of one emergent identity. In the context of CI and the state, memory would be replaced by institutions that allow for preserving past events. Those institutions could be law, jurisprudence, and legal and political history. The perception of different events could be transposed to constitutional moments, in which the state law is influenced, and public emotions stirred.[36] It is also

[31] ibid. 260.
[32] ibid.
[33] ibid. 261.
[34] ibid. 261–2.
[35] ibid. 261.
[36] András Sajó, "Emotions in constitutional design" (2010) 8 *International Journal of Constitutional Law* 354.

clear why based on those constitutional moments any sense of identity would arise—the sentiment behind all the historical events is a perfect explanation for why many social and legal actors attribute identity to the constitution. Respectively, unamendable norms are the core notion in the static concepts.[37] Those norms were anchored in the CI while being also an effect of interpreting the history by different actions, caused by the constitutional moments.

Finally, from the presented illusion of identity, one could follow into the current movements of abusive usage of CI—such as it takes place in Poland and Hungary.[38] What is not visible in trying to reconstruct the identity are social actors, of whom little seems to have similar goals and values. Dynamic concepts of Jacobsohn and Rosenfeld should be recalled here as a satisfactory explanation of how the identity emerges in the form of the constitutional subject as a result of the actions taken by the aforementioned actors.[39] However, this approach shouldn't totally undermine the concepts of normative approaches to constitutional identity presented in continental theory.[40] The danger appears when normative theories of identity mix with dynamic theories. For example, in the case K 3/21 Polish Constitutional Tribunal claimed that a part of national identity is constitutional identity and therefore one can infer parts of constitutional identity (such as boundaries of conferral of competences to the EU and unamendable norms) from the national identity.

4.2.2 Constitutional identity understood through Hobbes

Another philosopher with an outstanding and influential philosophy on the personhood of the state was Thomas Hobbes. His thought is widely known among political philosophers to be one of the sources for the sovereign.

37 Ziółkowski (n 1) 308.

38 Roger Daniel Kelemen and Laurent Pech, "The Uses and Abuses of Constitutional Pluralism: Undermining the Rule of Law in the Name of Constitutional Identity in Hungary and Poland" (2019) 21 *Cambridge Yearbook of European Legal Studies* 59.

39 Zoltán Szente, "Constitutional Identity as a Normative Constitutional Concept" (2022) 63 *Hungarian Journal of Legal Studies* 3.

40 Elke Cloots, "National Identity, Constitutional Identity, and Sovereignty in the EU" *(2016) 45 Netherlands Journal of Legal Philosophy* 82.

Although sovereignty is one of the parts of CI theories[41], especially the static ones, the Hobbesian approach to the notion will be mentioned only if necessary.

Hobbes defines a person as an entity "whose words or actions are considered, either as his own, or as representing the words or actions of any other man, or any other thing to whom they are attributed […]."[42] This quote would be sufficient to treat constitutional subjects as any other person, hence the subject is nothing more than a collective emergent speaking for all the unanimous and discorded voices. As it also appears, it is intuitive to treat CI in terms of personality. However, Hobbes in his magnum opus *Leviathan* distinguishes Persons into two types—natural person and artificial person. When the person is "considered as his owne, then is he called a Natural." A feigned, artificial person is understood as representing the words and actions of another, real person.[43] Representation is the center notion for Hobbes, as he derives it mostly from Greek (person as a mask) and Roman (person as outward appearance) traditions. Therefore, the person is always an actor on the stage, representing themself or others.[44] Representation can be also "truly or by fiction."[45] As Sean Fleming explains "natural persons are both representatives and representees."[46] The difference between being represented and representing is only relevant to artificial persons. A true artificial person is simultaneously a natural person. Fictional artificial persons are those who are not natural persons.[47] Despite this elaboration on the mentioned personality, Hobbes never provided a direct answer to the character of the state as a person. After considering the main arguments, Fleming concluded that the state, as pointed out by previous scholars, is an artificial person due to being represented by the assembly or public ministers.[48] Hence, as the assembly or the sovereign is

---

41 Thomas Hobbes, *Leviathan* (first published 1651, J. M. Dent & Sons, 1914) 83.

42 ibid.

43 ibid.

44 ibid.

45 ibid.

46 Sean Fleming, "The Two Faces of Personhood: Hobbes, Corporate Agency and the Personality of the State" (2021) 20 *European Journal of Political Theory* 8.

47 ibid. 14.

48 For example, the state is represented in international relations by the head of state or ministry of public affairs.

a representative, the state has a representative. According to Fleming, not only the state might not really be a fictional person but is a type of fictional character played by an artificial fictional person that is the assembly[49] emerging into the sovereign.

Understanding of the state and the role of different actors should be carried over to the constitution and its identity. What is more, the division into artificial, natural, fictional, and true persons is a useful tool. In dynamic theories, the constitutional subject would be one artificial fictional person, because it is always represented by different political options. As indicated, the subject is a dialectically emergent entity. Therefore, another question should be asked. As the constitutional subject always is represented, how—according to *the Leviathan*—does this subject emerge as a person from the collective? "A Multitude of men are made One Person, when they are by one man, or one Person, Represented."[50] What is more, Hobbes explains that if there are agreeing and disagreeing voices then "[…] the voyce of the greater number, must be considered as the voyce of them all."[51] Therefore, the constitutional subject lies with the majority.

Hobbesian reading of the CI showed that for the personality of constitutional subject a single majority voice is needed. What happens again with the abusive usage of the CI is that the majority option that speaks through the voices of constitutional courts, media, and parliament actually reads, interprets, and enforces specific understandings of CI. Again, if the CI is constructed by the voice of the majority, the static and dynamic concepts can be confused and unified standing for a singular theory, useful to justify any change in the national and international legal system.

The thoughts of Hume and Hobbes provide some insight into the forming of CI through the constitutional subject. According to the philosophers and mentioned literature, dynamic approaches might allow for a metaphorical, transpositional explanation for the emergence of abusive use of CI, highlighting the contents of static theories.

---

[49] The fiction of the assembly is that it speaks with one voice trough the collective decisions.

[50] Hobbes (n 41) 85.

[51] ibid.

4.3 Interpretation of constitutional identity using the theory of group identity by Roccas et al.

If we assume that the constitutional subject or CI is created by different identities, one may even argue that the choice of satisfactory interpretation of CI inside the constitutional subject can be explained by the psychology of identity. According to most theories of personal identity, people possess multiple identities.[52] The psychological explanations for how only one identity is represented at the time, mostly focus on the hierarchy of values or salience of identities. Take for example group identity theory proposed by Sonia Roccas et al. who proposed a four-dimensional model for the perception of group identity. Importance is connected with the perception of the ingroup. Commitment as a second dimension is understood as the means the person would use, even with sacrificing themself. Deference assumes the person would engage in group norms and actions despite the meaning of those norms and actions. The fourth dimension, which, according to researchers, is a natural consequence of dividing individuals into "us" and "them," is the sense of superiority. This entails the belief that one's group is better than others.[53]

If we apply these assumptions to the concepts of CI, the importance will indicate to what extent a given role is significant for the identity of the subject. When it comes to engagement, in this case, we would understand it as a change in the perception of certain constitutional ideals or the possibility of abandoning or reinterpreting certain characteristics of the constitution's principles or ideals. An example of a change in the dimension of engagement in European integration, and thus engagement in the group identity of European constitutions, is the difference between the approach taken by the constitution maker in the situation of amending the Constitution of the Republic of Poland to introduce the institution of the European Arrest Warrant and the one that, several years later, led to the declaration of a contradiction between

---

52 Not to be confused with dissociative identity disorder and multiple personalities disorder, for example, Sonia Roccas et al., "Toward a Unifying Model of Identification with Groups. Integrating Theoretical Perspectives" (2008) 12 *Personality and Social Psychology Review* 280; Henri Tajfel, "Social Identity and Intergroup Behaviour" *Fondation Maison des Sciences de l'Homme* 7; Peter J Burke and Jan E. Stets, *Identity Theory* (OUP 2009).

53 Roccas et al. (n 52), 280.

the Polish Constitution and the Treaty on European Union[54] or the European Convention on Human Rights,[55] leading to a disregard of the provisions of these international agreements. The issue of deference to the group and its values looks the same. The same goes for the sense of superiority, especially when the identity subject begins to perceive themselves through the lens of populist or abusive criteria.

4.4 Conclusions and possible research avenues

As the actors can read the constitution by themselves and provide different meanings influencing unamendable norms to their wishes. In the best of all possible worlds, the concept of CI should be abandoned within the static understanding of the notion as an opportunity to legitimize any constitutional abusive interpretation of the law. However, if the notion of the CI is going to remain, static theories should be interpreted in a closed system of the legal doctrine without any references to the dynamic theories. Static theories answer the question of "what are legal components of CI." Dynamic theories answer the question of "why there are different components of CI" or even "why there is CI." The multiple roles of actors emerging into the constitutional subject, allow for the use of hermeneutics to better understand the notion of CI. This opens up a field of study for empirical qualitative research methods, that can be applied in social sciences. For example, data analysis methods that are excellent for studying the phenomena of CI are thematic analysis, critical discourse analysis, and grounded theory.

The division proposed by Ziółkowski[56] seems to be useful, when only treated as a strict dichotomy. Dynamic approaches should be a field of study only for sociology, psychology, and political sciences as static understandings should be a field of study only for legal sciences. Tor the most reliable and valid research results, static and dynamic understandings should never be confused and mixed. The conclusion from the comparison of the constitutional subject to identity and personality theories proposed by Hume,

---

54 Polish Constitutional Tribunal Decision K 3/21.

55 Polish Constitutional Tribunal Decision K 6/21.

56 Ziółkowski (n 1).

Hobbes, and Roccas is that the constitutional subject is always constructed[57] within different legal actors, and therefore it has questionable ontological status and limited—if any—transposability to the law. As it is remarkable in the contemporary discourse, more scholars are seeing the obvious dangers of CI.[58] Therefore, if someone wants to maintain the notion, then the dichotomous treatment is advised.

Bibliography

Burke P. J. and Stets E. J., *Identity Theory* (OUP 2009).

Cloots E., "National Identity, Constitutional Identity, and Sovereignty in the EU" (2016) 45 *Netherlands Journal of Legal Philosophy* 82.

Demczuk A., "Tożsamość Człowieka jako Punkt Wyjścia dla Rozumienia Tożsamości Konstytucyjnej. Wybrane Koncepcje Filozoficzne i Psychologiczne" in Monika Florczak-Wątor and Marcin Krzemiński (eds), *Interdyscyplinarny Wymiar Tożsamości Konstytucyjnej.*

Fabbrini F. and Sajó A., "The dangers of constitutional identity" (2018) 25 *European Law Journal* 457.

Fleming S., "The Two Faces of Personhood: Hobbes, Corporate Agency and the Personality of the State" (2021) 20 *European Journal of Political Theory* 8.

Freud S., *Loss of Reality* (1924).

Hobbes T., *Leviathan.* (first published 1651, J. M. Dent & Sons LTD 1914).

Hume D., *Treatise of Human Nature* (first published 1739–40, Clarendon Press 1896).

Jacobsohn G. J., *Constitutional Identity* (Harvard University Press 2010).

Kelemen R. D. and Pech L., "The Uses and Abuses of Constitutional Pluralism: Undermining the Rule of Law in the Name of Constitutional

57 Monika Polzin, "Constitutional Identity, Unconstitutional Amendments and the Idea of Constituent Power: The Development of the Doctrine of Constitutional Identity in German Constitutional Law" (2016) 14 *International Journal of Constitutional Law* 411.

58 Fabbrini and Sajó (n 22) 82.

Identity in Hungary and Poland" (2019) 21 *Cambridge Yearbook of European Legal Studies* 59.

Polzin M., "Constitutional Identity, Unconstitutional Amendments and the Idea of Constituent Power: The development of the doctrine of constitutional identity in German constitutional law" (2016) 14 *International Journal of Constitutional Law* 411.

Roccas S., Sagiv L., Schwartz S., Halevy N. and Eidelson R., "Toward a Unifying Model of Identification with Groups. Integrating Theoretical Perspectives" (2008) 12 *Personality and Social Psychology Review* 280.

Rosenfeld M., *The Identity of the Constitutional Subject. Selfhood, Citizenship, Culture and Community* (Routledge 2010).

Sajó A., "Emotions in constitutional design" (2010) 8 *International Journal of Constitutional Law* 354.

Szente Z., "Constitutional Identity as a Normative Constitutional Concept" (2022) 63 *Hungarian Journal of Legal Studies* 3.

Śledzińska-Simon A., "Constitutional identity in 3D: A model of individual, relational, and collective self and its application in Poland" (2015) 13 *International Journal of Constitutional Law* 124.

Śledzińska-Simon A., Koncepcja Tożsamości Konstytucyjnej: Wymiar Indywidualny, Relatywny oraz Zbiorowy (2016) *Acta Universitatis Wratislaviensis* 335.

Śledzińska-Simon A. and Ziółkowski M., *Constitutional Identity of Poland: Is the Emperor Putting on the Old Clothes of Sovereignty?* (2017) <https://dx.doi.org/10.2139/ssrn.2997407>.

Tajfel H., "Social Identity and Intergroup Behaviour" (1974) 13 *Fondation Maison des Sciences de l"Homme* 7.

Zagaria A., Ando A. and Zennaro A., "Psychology: A Giant with Feet of Clay" (2020) 54 *Integrative Psychological and Behavioral Science* 521.

Ziółkowski M., "Dwie Płaszczyzny Dyskusji o Tożsamości Konstytucyjnej (Teoria versus Dogmatyka)" in Andrzej Wróbel and Michał Ziółkowski (eds), *Tożsamość Konstytucyjna w Wybranych Państwach Członkowskich Unii Europejskiej*. Wolters Kluwer 2021.

Constitutional Identities in Central and Eastern Europe: The Periphery Paradox

Jozef Jenčík

ABSTRACT

This chapter explores the complex interplay of constitutional identities in Central and Eastern Europe, characterized as the "Periphery Paradox." Rooted in Oswald Spengler's *The Decline of the West*, it dissects the core-periphery dynamic using Hegelian paradoxes. Specifically, it highlights Hegel's paradox where history is shaped by "slaves" rather than "masters," emphasizing that freedom arises from the toils of "slaves" rather than the rule of "masters." The chapter delves into Hegel's profound influence on Ľudovít Štúr and the Slovak national awakening, underscoring Štúr's pivotal role in preserving the Slovak identity during the nineteenth century. In the backdrop of the contemporary West's decline, the Periphery Paradox gains added complexity. The chapter navigates the potential risks of unharmonious coexistence between the West's lifeless technocratic core and the Central and Eastern European states' emergent constitutional identities, driven by a fervent desire for distinctiveness. Without alignment, the specter of a dystopian future, akin to the logic of the core-periphery concept, threatens the state regimes of Western civilization. This exploration seeks a balanced path, respecting periphery constitutional identities while adapting to the challenges of Western decline.

Keywords: core-periphery concept, Periphery Paradox, Spengler, Hegel, Štúr, mnemonic constitutionalism, technocracy

5.1 Prologue

In the present chapter, I would like to follow up on my dissertation thesis, *The Future of State Regimes: Dystopia and Antiutopia (Cultural and Theory-of-State Approach)*,[1] to understand the important dynamics behind constitutional identities in Central and Eastern Europe: The Periphery Paradox.

In my dissertation thesis, I introduced a theory of dystopia as a predictive model based on Spengler's *The Decline of the West*, which was verified by an analysis of dystopian and antiutopian literature of the twentieth and twenty-first centuries and by an analysis of contemporary political *praxis*.

1 Jozef Jenčík, "*The Future of State Regimes: Dystopia and Antiutopia (Cultural and Theory-of-State Approach)*" (Univerzita Komenského v Bratislave PraF 2022) 242 <https://opac.crzp.sk/?fn=detailBiblioForm&sid=9F4A0969CCDCF40EDE9C471EA833> accessed October 15, 2023.

The analysis was based on a sample of dystopian and antiutopian literature of the twentieth and twenty-first centuries (Zamjatin's *We* 1920, Huxley's *Brave New World* 1932, Orwell's *1984* [1948], Rand's *Atlas Shrugged* 1957, Kafka's *The Trial* 1915, Atwood's *The Handmaid's Tale* 1986, and Eggers' *The Circle* 2013) and was focused on the empiric verification of these evolutionary tendencies of dystopic regimes:

i. state ideology of the scientific type,
ii. nationwide control of the population,
iii. disrupting market economy principles,
iv. normalization of the state of exception and
v. politicizing healthcare.

I explained that all these tendencies point to the decline of the West and show us *deficiently* the urgent need for a new political order that would rethink the concept of individual human rights and liberties as collective rights, the free-market economy as a shared economy, and representative democracy as a participatory endeavor.

5.2 Spengler's postulations and findings

These hypotheses were inspired by Spengler's postulations and findings in his famous *The Decline of the West*, as he explained the ever-problematic relations between necessity/freedom, technique/human dignity, power/democracy, and history/thinking in a thought-provoking manner. His starting points, as well as his conclusions, inspired many philosophers and thinkers of the twentieth century, notably Martin Heidegger.

In an already dystopic fashion he stated—as a matter of fact—that Western civilization is irresistibly coming to its end and that trying to avoid it would lead to a society without the ability to think—a dystopic society:

> The one who does not understand that this conclusion (the decline of Western Civilization, author's note) is obligatory for us and unmodifiable, that our choice is either to think decline or not to think at all, between accepting this fate, or despairing of the future and life; one who cannot feel the magnificence even in the realization of powerful intelligences, in energy and the discipline of metal-hard natures, in battles fought by the coldest and by the most abstract means; one who is obsessed with provincial idealism and who would prefer to follow the ways of

> life of past ages—he must give up all desire to understand history, live historically or create history.[2]

Within the fundamental-ontological analysis of the dystopian development of the state regimes of Western civilization, I described three ontologically fundamental phenomena that make the dystopia *necessary if* no political action toward re-thinking the declining political order of the West is taken:

i. the phenomenon of modern "Faustian" technology,[3]
ii. the phenomenon of *the intervention of abstract truths in the world of facts*,[4] and
iii. the phenomenon of *the non-obvious basis of political tradition*.[5]

Against the misinterpretation of Spengler's worldview that Western technique is evil or even the cause of a Western dystopic future, I explained, on the contrary, that Western technique is the only factor that could lead to an alternative and more meaningful future. According to Spengler, the failure of scientific symbolism at the stage of the ongoing decline of Western culture is only covered by the perfect mastery of "Faustian" science in experimental technique.[6] Whereas, therefore, abstract scientific knowledge—precisely because of its abstractness, which is never identical with life—is never true. Technology, on the other hand, is always true because its concepts are instrumental means rather than ends in themselves. Thus, in a time of decline in which life once again asserts its unquestionable claim on Western civilization, the leading historical role is played by the modern "Faustian" technique, which is compatible with life thanks to its instrumental character. However, the conscious use of technology can no longer belong to scientists whose dogmatic foundations are shaken by the demands of life but to thinkers whose

2 Oswald Spengler, *The Decline of the West* (1st edn, Vintage Books Inc. 2006) 29.
3 ibid. 409–15.
4 ibid. 365 et subseq.
5 ibid. 370.
6 ibid. 260–1.

thinking can withstand the suddenly changing reality of life. Only on this basis could Heidegger analyze the end of philosophy and the role of thinking.[7]

However, Spengler was already aware that thinking is very difficult for a "Faustian" person precisely because of his cultural affiliation. A classical person could think freely, but he did not consider it necessary, while a "Faustian" person wants to think freely but cannot because he thinks only according to order, and only in order does he find his sense of freedom.[8] Martin Heidegger systematically understood these observations of the historian in his famous thesis from the lecture *What is called thinking?*—"The most presumptuous thing in our presumptuous age is that we do not yet think."[9] For Spengler, the source of this difficulty lies in the culturally unprecedented phenomenon of the intervention of abstract truths into the world of facts, which just rests on the assumption that abstract truths (be they dogmatic truths of science or dogmatic truths of laws) intervene in the world of facts in order to dominate life with its escalating demands on declining Western civilization (e.g., domination of cities over countryside, influence of written books on politics, etc.). According to Heidegger, this culturally conditioned givenness of the "Faustian" person is a consequence of the modern "Faustian" technique:

> [...] by a suitable combination of logistics with modern psychology, psychoanalysis, and sociology, the concern of future philosophy will become perfect. However, this encirclement of thought is not human work. Rather, these disciplines consist of a lot of power that comes from afar and for which the Greek words poetry and technique are perhaps still appropriate names, provided that they name us thinkers what we are supposed to think.[10]

For Spengler, breaking the "thread" of political tradition is a manifestation of the phenomenon of the intervention of abstract truths in the world of facts. According to Spengler, Robespierre and Napoleon failed in the establishment of a political tradition because they found nothing around them or in

---

7 Martin Heidegger, *Konec filosofie a* úkol *myšlení* (3th edn, Oikúmené 2021). On the impact of Heidegger's work on the doctrine of democracy and the rule of law, see Gianni Vattimo, "The End of Philosophy in the Age of Democracy" (2006) 18 Portique <https://journals.openedition.org/leportique/pdf/811> accessed October 15, 2023.

8 Spengler (n 2) 395.

9 Martin Heidegger, *Co znamená myslet?* (1st edn, Oikúmené 2014) 9.

10 ibid. 17.

themselves, which would be the self-evident basis essential to the creation of any new creation.[11] Spengler hoped that perhaps with the contribution of the remnants of the political tradition from the pre-revolutionary period, a political tradition would be created again in the state regimes in the future, which the ζῷον πολιτικόν could follow up on again with its activities. However, his hopes were not fulfilled, as instead totalitarianism of the twentieth century—Nazism and Bolshevism—arose. Instead of the political tradition, they heavily relied on the novel form of a government—methods of ideology and terror. Hannah Arendt, in her thought-provoking analysis, predicted that more authentic forms of method and terror would only come in the future.[12] More authentic means that they are not perceived as something brutal but more like the standard way of organizing the public. However, the inability to think does not result from the totalitarianism of the twentieth century—Nazism and Bolshevism—but from the modern "Faustian" technique, whose authentic political manifestation is the rational-utilitarian doctrine of the Welfare State. Hannah Arendt therefore constantly emphasized, in contrast to the abstract maxim of quantitative utilitarianism, "the greatest happiness for the greatest possible number of people," that a person can be happy only when at least once he thinks about what it actually means to be happy.[13] According to Spengler, the idea of human dignity is the result of the action of machines on "Faustian" man; it is for the good of the machine that human life has become precious.[14] The continued decline of Western civilization in the twenty-first century thus needs to be thought through the "Faustian" technique, as the source of human dignity cannot continue to be ignored like in totalitarian movements of the twentieth century, such as Nazism and Bolshevism, whose ideologies relied on the past, or so-called provincial thinking. If the ζῷον πολιτικό fails in this defined task, they will have to put up with such an order of power that it will seem to them that his own modern "Faustian" technology has taken over. They will have to come to terms with the power order in which they normalize the state of emergency because it failed to establish a new sovereign order of power. They will have to come

[11] Spengler (n 2) 370.

[12] Hannah Arendt, *The Origins of Totalitarianism* (first published 1951, The World Publishing Company 1962).

[13] Hannah Arendt, *Vita activa* (2nd edn, Oikúmené 2009) 396.

[14] Spengler (n 2) 411.

to terms with the order of power, whose internal authority—efficiency—is built on the methods of ideology and terror.

5.3 The (Western) concept of core-periphery as based on fundamental-ontological analysis of the dystopian development of the state regimes of Western civilization

The concept of core-periphery in the Western context represents a fundamental model for understanding the global distribution of power, resources, and knowledge, as the influence of Western civilization has *finally* spread all over the world. In this paradigm, the "core" signifies the dominant, central regions or countries, while the "periphery" comprises the less developed or subordinate regions. This model extends far beyond geography, influencing various aspects of our society, from politics to knowledge systems.

Based on Spengler's postulations and findings, it is clear how it is founded on the fundamental-ontological analysis of the dystopian development of the state regimes of Western civilization:

i. the idea of sovereignty,
ii. monotheistic religions,
iii. the dogmatic character of knowledge, and
iv. modernity.

At the heart of the Western concept of periphery is the idea of sovereignty. The core, often Western countries, have historically asserted their sovereignty over both their internal affairs and external interactions. According to Spengler, sovereignty is the life symbol of such an established—first order, not some fictitious concept. It distinguishes between subjects and objects. A possible overthrow of authority can never replace it with a new one, but it throws the entire order of power into politics, which is alienated from it.[15] In Western culture, which is inherently intolerant, sovereignty translates into the ability to dictate the terms of global discourse, establish international institutions,

[15] ibid. 361.

and influence the fate of peripheral nations. While classical culture had tolerance in its essence (tolerance of different opinions, etc.), Western culture, with its monotheistic religion and the dogmatic character of modern "Faustian" knowledge, must first learn tolerance.[16]

Furthermore, monotheistic religions originating in the West, such as Christianity, have played a significant role in shaping the core-periphery relationship. These religions, through their missionary activities and their influence on moral and ethical values, have often been instruments of cultural and ideological dominance. The intolerance of Western culture thus epitomizes not only in relations of power, where war is its natural habitat, but also on the charity level, where love presides. There is natural intolerance in Western culture without the slightest doubt. As an example *par excellence*, we can cite J. Locke, who, in his *Letter Concerning Toleration* (1689), expresses the opinion that atheists must be excluded from his liberal concept of the social contract at all costs because atheists are said to hold nothing holy.[17] Locke's opinion is applied in a secularized form in Western civilization to this day: the credibility of the population of state regimes must be verified by a valid identity document at all costs.

The dogmatic character of knowledge is another key element in this paradigm. Western epistemology has often been regarded as the authoritative source of knowledge, shaping our understanding of science, philosophy, and even history. This authority sometimes leads to a Eurocentric view of knowledge, marginalizing alternative perspectives from the periphery.

The core dominance also expresses itself through the term modern, which, for Spengler, is the last and final term of Western culture. Spengler predicted that the term modern will be stretched to its limit, where it will no longer last.[18] The later historical development of Western civilization showed that this term has endured more than Spengler assumed at the beginning of the twentieth century. We could really feel the signs of the period of state and law, devoid of any form, predicted by Spengler, only with the arrival of postmodern philosophy, which, however, is still (as the name suggests) essentially intended for the modern, even if it is already trying to detach itself from it.

---

16 ibid. 208.

17 John Locke, *Dopis o toleranci* (first published 1689, Atlantis 2000) 82.

18 Spengler (n 2) 15.

We can therefore consider postmodernism as a symbolic sign of a nascent culture, which, however, has not yet found its ground.

In practice, the core-periphery concept is evident in the global economic system, where core countries control the flow of capital and resources, exploiting periphery nations for their benefit. It is visible in international politics, with powerful countries dictating the terms of diplomacy, trade, and conflict resolution. In the realm of knowledge, it reflects in the dominance of Western theories and ideologies, often marginalizing indigenous or non-Western perspectives.

In summary, the Western concept of the core and periphery is not only a geographical model but a comprehensive framework that underscores the distribution of power, sovereignty, knowledge, and culture on a global scale. It's a lens through which we can examine the persistent dynamics of domination and subordination in our interconnected world. ζῷον πολιτικό must learn to reflect this unfreedom in Western civilization if he wants to live in a democratic and legal—free state.

5.3.1 Periphery in Hegel's philosophy (1770–1831)

In other words, the imaginative appropriation of the necessary (oppressive) is the condition of the possible (free). Arguably, the greatest pioneer of this thinking in Western philosophy was Georg Wilhelm Friedrich Hegel, who took the dogmatic, systematic stance—so typical of Western knowledge but fulfilled it with notions that contradicted the usual meaning in a paradoxical manner. What was first experienced with disinclination as something dead-handed, fogyish, obscurant, retrograde, or retrogressive was then valued as something that possessed enormous value, even making the periphery the core value of Western society. He even explored the possibility of the new logic, dialectic, which is very simply presented to students as thesis + antithesis—synthesis. Solomon has thus argued that by incorporating the very contradictions of Western cultural heritage into *one* synthetic philosophy, he has "finished" traditional Western philosophy—epistemology—and opened the door for contemporary speculative philosophy, postmodern philosophy, philosophy of language, and deconstruction.[19]

---

[19] See closer Robert Solomon, "Hegel's Epistemology" (1971) American Philosophical Quarterly 11 (4) 277.

Two of the main statements of his philosophy, the most paradoxical and breath-taking, we can deduce from his works as follows:

The source of all history stems from the slaves and not from the masters.

The source of all freedom stems from the slaves' work, not from the masters'.

By recognizing the slaves' work as a main contribution to all history and freedom, he completely perverted the classical cultural heritage and contributed to their gradual liberation.[20] Through his philosophy of spirit, he even inspired many peripheric nations to incite the so-called awakening movements and standardize their mother languages. And indeed, being one of the most prominent representatives of Western philosophy, Georg Wilhelm Friedrich Hegel deeply influenced the Slavs in Central and Eastern Europe, mainly through Ľudovít Štúr[21] who was one of the most influential names in the Slovak national awakening due to his pivotal role in standardizing the Slovak language and his active involvement in both cultural and political aspects of the awakening. The Slovak Republic has a state hymn with the strong motive of awakening even to these days in the form of Janko Matúška's poem, who was Štúr's great sympathizer. Therefore, it is not surprising that to him is attributed the prediction that the spirit, with its necessity, will shift to Slavic nations in the future.

5.3.2 L'udovít Štúr and his political use of periphery (1848/1849)

As the revolutionary spirit of 1848 reverberated across Europe, Štúr recognized that to resist the assimilation into the Hungarian core, he needed to adroitly harness the structures of the periphery. Štúr's political program, while bearing modern elements such as the pursuit of national liberation, exhibited a multifaceted reliance on the periphery. Hegel's dialectical approach and philosophical outlook played a significant role in shaping Štúr's thinking. His approach was pragmatic, recognizing that in the geopolitical landscape of the nineteenth century, the periphery could serve as a safeguard against assimilation into the dominant core. One of the most intriguing examples

---

[20] Georg Wilhelm Friedrich Hegel, *The Philosophy of History* (1st edn, P. F. Collier and Son 1901) 157.

[21] Emerich Coreth, Peter Ehlen, Josef Schmidt, *Filosofie 19. století* (1st edn, Nakladatelství Olomouc 2003) 92–3.

of this is his approach to Emperor Franz Joseph I as his strategy emphasized the peripheric element of imperial authority. Štúr understood that, within the Habsburg Empire, the periphery could provide a counterbalance to the Hungarian core's influence. By appealing to the monarch's goodwill and protection, Štúr sought to secure the rights and autonomy of the Slovak people. Here we encounter one layer of the core-periphery concept.

In this intricate dance between the core and periphery, Štúr's strategy also draws upon the influence of Russian authors. Their literary and philosophical contributions significantly impacted his intellectual development. The Russian periphery, in this context, enriched Štúr's worldview with ideas and narratives that extended beyond the Hungarian core's dominance. The allegorical form in which Štúr infuses the national spirit takes the form of a woman, a multiple mother, like a Matryoshka doll. Outwardly unhappy, immersed in eternal sadness over ruins and ruins, but the deeper inside, the more vital and popular it is. Such an allegory of a mother who gives birth, cries, and dies corresponds to the revivalist form of Slovak national art. Only when the poet wraps her in the mantle of Slavophile ideology and combines Herder's and Kollár's vision of Slavs with a romantic understanding of humanity does the mother begin not only to live but also to give life, according to a higher national morality. In the poetry of Ľudovít Štúr, the romantic cult of the people in connection with the Slavophile ideology becomes a guarantor of the existence of the Slovak nation, as well as a chance for the original peripheral space, transferred to the center of national life, to become the birthplace of a new national leader who will restore both memory and space.[22]

In summary, Štúr's political use of the periphery, in conjunction with Hegelian and Russian influence, epitomizes the multifaceted nature of the core-periphery concept. It underlines the strategic interplay between core and periphery and the intellectual amalgamation of core philosophy with peripheric political maneuvering. In the historical episode of Štúr's activism, we find a profound example of how culture, philosophy, and geopolitics converge in the complex interplay between core and periphery.

---

[22] Marian Bodnár (ed.), *Dejiny filozofického myslenia na Slovensku* (1st edn, Veda, vydavateľstvo Slovenskej akadémie vied 1987) 357.

5.3.3 Central and Eastern Europe (CEE) and its contemporary political use of periphery

Emerging constitutional identities in Central and Eastern Europe are still at the beginning of the twenty-first century, a pending element of the discourse that, after the Velvet Revolution in late 1989, was almost exclusively centered around democracy, human rights and freedoms, free market economies, and European integration.

There is something paradoxical in that the dominance of Western liberal democracy celebrated its greatest victories when it was already quite exhausted in its internal possibilities of development. Nevertheless, the Slovak Republic, among other peripheric countries, almost exclusively focused on getting access to the Western core, represented by the European Union (EU) and the North Atlantic Treaty Organization (NATO). The importance for the Slovak citizens' to access these organizations was self-evident; e.g., the only valid referendum of the Slovak Republic for which the quorum is the majority of all citizens was a referendum for access to the European Union.

However, as the unresolved need for transformation of the EU and NATO was raising her life-claims, the messianic dream of peripheric countries accessing artificial paradise has started to vanish. And as an active approach was required from the peripheral countries, they related their respective cultural and political traditions to counter what Jurgen Habermas called the lure of technocracy.[23]

The perfect example of this dynamic in the Slovak Republic is Róbert Fico. Slovakia, like other Central and Eastern European countries, aspired to further integrate into the core of the EU. This included participation in the Eurozone, which Slovakia adopted in 2009, and support for deeper economic and political integration within the EU. Róbert Fico, during his time as Prime Minister of Slovakia, generally expressed a pro-European Union (EU) stance. Fico was known for his pragmatic approach to EU affairs. He often focused on issues related to economic development, social policies, and regional cohesion. His government implemented policies aimed at reducing income inequality and increasing the living standards of ordinary citizens. In 2017, he declared that Slovakia must run into the core of the Union and not wait. This was announced on Wednesday before the two-day (June 22 and 23)

---

[23] See closer Jürgen Habermas, *The Lure of Technocracy* (1st edn, Polity Press 2015).

meeting of the European Council in Brussels on the grounds of the NR SR Committee for European Affairs.

However, in March 2018, Robert Fico's government faced significant public protests following the murder of investigative journalist Ján Kuciak and his fiancée. The protesters raised concerns about corruption and the rule of law in Slovakia. After stepping down as Prime Minister, Fico remained influential within the Smer-SD party and continued to play a pivotal role in Slovak politics, even in the governmental opposition, which, *inter alia*, promised the return of the rule of law. Paradoxically, the practice of using the penitent institute by the law enforcement authorities and the outbreak of exceptional pandemic measures made Róbert Fico the leading defender of human rights. There was a total of 32 decisions of the Constitutional Court of the Slovak Republic in proceedings initiated by a group of deputies for the SMER-SD party.

Considering the possibilities of applying the methods of ideology and terror in exceptional circumstances, Róbert Fico's pro-human rights stance was not unfounded.

The possibilities of applying the methods of ideology and terror when using the institute of the "penitent" (or cooperating accused)[24] are currently used in several Western countries. This development trend is a manifestation of the unsustainability of "normal" criminal proceedings, characterized by the presumption of innocence, the right to defense, and the protection of the basic rights of the accused. It is another confirmation of Spengler's decline of the West. As a method of terror, it manifests itself in the practical application of this institute when gross coercion is exerted on the accused in violation of these "normal" principles of criminal procedure by the law enforcement authorities. In the era of the decline of the West, this method shapes the state regime and ensures its basic functions, such as the safety of the population. This development trend is also politicized in Western states, where we can more and more often observe that the most successful political campaigns are largely centered around the suppression of crime, which would not be possible without the institution of the penitent. The danger of this method, however, is that it does not solve the causes of crime, which can paradoxically contribute to the preservation of a high level of

[24] Criminal Procedure Code 2005, § 218.

crime in the state regimes of the West. In fact, as Judge Šramko pointed out in his professional article,[25] the application of the institute of the penitent under the conditions of the Slovak Republic took on the religious features of worshipping a kind of "penitent" cult.

The possibilities of applying the method of ideology and terror when using state of exception measures are also used in several Western countries. Specifically, for example, Agamben correctly stated[26] in his comparison that the measures adopted on the basis of the COVID-19 pandemic with their pretext of protecting public health were able to limit the personal freedom of the population of the modern state to an extent that had no parallel even in the totalitarianism of the twentieth century, but this unprecedented restriction in the case of pandemic measures pursued legitimate objectives. However, the question remains whether these legitimate goals in specific cases could justify interference with human rights under a strict test of proportionality. For example, in the Slovak Republic, the Constitutional Court of the Slovak Republic deemed some exceptional pandemic provisions unconstitutional.[27]

However, Róbert Fico's pro-human rights stance was combined with Euroskeptic political currents, as many of them gained their respective voices in Central and Eastern European countries. Fico is a palpable admirer of the "sovereign" politics of Viktor Orbán, which uses national tradition to counterbalance the lifeless measures of the technocratic European Union. Róbert Fico, as a pragmatist, is certainly not against membership in the European Union or NATO, but he emphasizes the need to protect Slovak interests. To that end, he even renamed his party SMER-SD to SMER-SSD to emphasize the national character of his social policy. Taking Viktor Orbán as a role model, he shall certainly be willing to use so-called mnemonic constitutionalism, whose tools have common characteristics with the basic unit of the method of ideology, that is, a password or slogan. Its strength in the context of mnemonic constitutionalism rests on the genealogical feeling of Western

---

25 Peter Šamko, "Kult kajúcnika ako trend roku 2020 alebo čo nás môže naučiť prípad prokurátora JUDr. Jozefa Mamráka" (*Právne listy*, December 29, 2020) <http://www.pravnelisty.sk/clanky/a914-kult-kajucnika-ako-trend-roku-2020-alebo-co-nas-moze-naucit-pripad-prokuratora-judr-jozefa-mamraka> accessed October 15, 2023.

26 Giorgio Agamben, *Where Are We Now? The Epidemic as Politics* (1st ed., Rowman & Littlefield 2021) 9.

27 *Public Defender of Rights* v *Slovak Republic* [2021] PL ÚS 4/2021-136.

man, which Spengler so succinctly described in his work *The Decline of the West*. As a method of terror, it can manifest itself in a deficient mode of this feeling, in which historical facts from the domain of historical sciences no longer mean anything to the population and are instead standardized by the legislator or even the constitution maker. As a rule, however, states normalize historical facts in a politically overcome dichotomy of "us" and "them," in which "our" nation is either an innocent victim or a glorious freedom fighter against a hostile aggressor. In the case of interference with freedom of expression, the result is often a not-inconsiderable interference with scientific freedom of expression and the repression of the population by means of criminal law. Such use of symbolism by the state regimes of the Council of Europe, within the framework of dystopian constitutionalism,[28] was also currently addressed by the ECtHR in the case of *Dr. Perinček* v. *Switzerland* [2015] 27510/08, in which the ECtHR took the questions of qualification of the Armenian Genocide away from state monopoly and left them to historians and civil society. However, the justification of this decision left many lawyers on edge when the ECtHR distinguished the Armenian Genocide from the Holocaust as a kind of privileged genocide, thus trivializing the suffering of millions of Armenians in the Ottoman Empire. In the case of the Slovak Republic, as an example that goes beyond the scope of freedom of expression, we can cite Act No. 283/2021 Coll. on the withdrawal of undeserved benefits from representatives of the communist regime, which was challenged in the Constitutional Court of the Slovak Republic and was suspended on March 21, 2022, in decision *Group of 31 members of the National Council of the Slovak Republic* v *Slovak Republic* [2022] PL ÚS 2/2022-14.

5.4 Conclusion

In the period of Western decline, the periphery paradox is even more paradoxical: there is an imminent danger of a willingness to stay in the periphery forever.

On the one hand, we have a Western lifeless core that manifests itself as the lure of technocracy, and on the other, we have awakening constitutional

[28] See closer Thomas Crocker, 'Dystopian Constitutionalism' (2015) Journal of Constitutional Law 18 (2) 593.

identities in Central and Eastern Europe with the willingness to give its states a life form.

If no intersection between these tendencies is found in the longer term, there is a greater danger of completing the dystopian development of the state regimes of Western civilization, akin to the logic of the core-periphery concept.

With the postmodern shift unavoidable as a sign of Western decline, it is therefore argued that the most urgent challenge in forming constitutional identities in Central and Eastern Europe is to find so-called mnemonic constitutionalism effective beyond mere state reprisals. If succeeded, the periphery paradox with its lure on nations of Central and Eastern Europe to stay in the "periphery" of the European Union could be finally escaped, as it would undoubtedly be a pattern worth following even for Western core members.

Bibliography

Agamben G., *Homo sacer* (1st ed, Oikúmené 2011) 192.

———, *Where Are We Now? The Epidemic as Politics* (1st ed, Rowman & Littlefield 2021) 106.

Arendt H., *Between Past and Future* (first published 1961, Penguin Books 2006) 266.

———, *The Origins of Totalitarianism* (first published 1951, The World Publishing Company 1962) 554.

———, *Vita activa* (2nd ed, Oikúmené 2009) 396.

Atwood M., *The Handmaid's Tale* (Vintage Classics, Random House UK 2010) 334.

Bilińska I., "Formy národného priestoru v poézií Ľudovíta Štúra' in Peter Zajac (ed.) *Štúr, štúrovci, romantici a obrodenci* (1st ed, Ústav slovenskej literatúry SAV 2016) 456.

Burns P. R., *Kafka's Law. The Trial and American Criminal Justice* (1st edn, The University of Chicago Press 2014) 190.

Bodnár M. (ed.), *Dejiny filozofického myslenia na Slovensku* (1st edn, Veda, vydavateľstvo Slovenskej akadémie vied 1987) 490.

Buchwalter A. (ed.), *Hegel and Global Justice* (Studies in Global Justice, vol. 10, Springer 2012) 249.

Coreth E., Ehlen P., Schmidt J., *Filosofie 19. století* (1st edn, Nakladatelství Olomouc 2003) 224.

Crocker T., "Dystopian Constitutionalism" (2015) Journal of Constitutional Law 18 (2) 593.

Eggers D., *The Circle* (1st ed, Penguin Books 2014) 512.

Fukuyama F., *The End of History and the Last Man* (first published 1992, Penguin 2020) 464.

Habermas J., *The Lure of Technocracy* (1st ed, Polity Press 2015) 176.

Heidegger M., *Co znamená myslet?* (Petr Fischer & Ivan Chvatík tr, 1st ed, Oikúmené 2014) 60.

———, *Konec filosofie a úkol myšlení* (Ivan Chvatík tr, 3th ed, Oikúmené 2021) 64.

———, *Pathmarks* (1st ed, Cambridge University Press 1998) 385.

Hegel G. W. F., *Hegel's Science of Logic* (1st edn, Allen & Unwin 1969) 845.

———, *Outlines of the Philosophy of Right* (Oxford World's Classics edn, Oxford University Press 2008) 432.

———, *The Philosophy of History* (1st edn, P. F. Collier and Son 1901) 157.

Huxley A., *Brave New World* (first published 1932, Vintage Publishing 2011) 288.

Jenčík J., "*The Future of State Regimes: Dystopia and Antiutopia (Cultural and Theory-of-State Approach)*" (Univerzita Komenského v Bratislave PraF 2022) 242 <https://opac.crzp.sk/?fn=detailBiblioForm&sid=9F4A0969C-CDCF40EDE9C471EA833> accessed October 15, 2023.

Kafka F., *The Trial* (Cornell University ed, Schocken Books 1999) 312.

Locke J., *Dopis o toleranci* (Petr Horak tr, first published 1689, Atlantis 2000) 103.

Orwell G., *1984* (first published 1948, Random House 1998) 325.

Rand A., *Atlas Shrugged* (first published 1957, Penguin Books 1997) 1079.

Rousseau J., *The Social Contract* (Oxford World's Classics edn, Oxford University Press 1999) 216.

Solomon R., "Hegel's Epistemology" (1971) American Philosophical Quarterly 11 (4) 277.

Spengler O., *The Decline of the West* (1st ed, Vintage Books 2006) 450.

Šamko P., "Kult kajúcnika ako trend roku 2020 alebo čo nás môže naučiť prípad prokurátora JUDr. Jozefa Mamráka" (*Právne listy*, December 29, 2020) <http://www.pravnelisty.sk/clanky/a914-kult-kajucnika-ako-trend-roku-2020-alebo-co-nas-moze-naucit-pripad-prokuratora-judr-jozefa-mamraka> accessed October 15, 2023.

Vattimo G., "The End of Philosophy in the Age of Democracy" (2006) 18 Portique <https://journals.openedition.org/leportique/pdf/811> accessed October 15, 2023.

Zamjatin J., *We* (1st edn, Sahara Publisher Books 1924) 204.

On Power, Violence, and Judicial Activism in Poland: The Janus-Faced Judiciary[1]

Piotr Zaleski

ABSTRACT
This chapter addresses the issue of lawmaking culture through the lens of different traditional understandings of political power. Hannah Arendt's theoretical framework is introduced to highlight the distinction between the Hebrew-Christian, command-oriented tradition and the Greco-Roman, community-oriented tradition of political power. The chapter suggests a connection between these traditions and judicial activism and restraint, respectively. It also emphasizes the importance of republican ideals in Poland's political tradition, while exploring the potential incongruence between these ideals and the contemporary liberal approach to the judiciary's role in political life. This demonstrates the Janus-faced nature of the contemporary Polish Constitutional Judiciary—caught between its republican heritage and liberal influences.

Keywords: judicial activism, political power, constitutional adjudication, republicanism, lawmaking culture

6.1 Introduction

The post-communist transformation in Central and Eastern Europe has been interpreted by some as a true generational success and by others as a traumatic failure. Its impact on Poland's contemporary legal, economic and political system is undeniable, and the task of summarizing all its effects seems, at least so far, unattainable. Various social scientists have struggled to grasp some aspects of the transformation, while inevitably overlooking others. As a result, the transformation remains somewhat of a mystery, and its consequences are yet to be understood in their entirety.[2]

While some implications of the transformation remain hidden, others are relatively obvious, and few more so than those in the legislative process. From the one-party system, the so-called proletarian democracy, countries such as Poland transformed themselves into, at least nominally, liberal democracies.

---

[1] I would like to convey my gratitude to Dr. Michal Dudek at the Faculty of Law, Jagiellonian University, for his extensive lectures on political power were tremendously inspiring in the writing of this chapter.

[2] Grzegorz Ekiert, "Prawidłowości transformacji w Europie Wschodniej" (2011) 1 *Studia Socjologiczne*.

They were deeply inspired by post-war constitutionalism, neoliberal economics, and the human rights doctrine. The transition process itself was not always smooth, but generally led to the creation of functioning (if sometimes flawed) constitutional orders. The liberal-democratic legislative process was to be at the heart of the new order.

In this essay I will argue that the post-communist transformation in Poland (and perhaps in other Central and Eastern European countries) has created a specific culture of lawmaking. By a culture of lawmaking, I mean that there is a specific set of social attitudes regarding how legal rules are enacted. It is completely indifferent to the content of these regulations and is concerned only with the process itself. I believe that the culture of lawmaking affects the social reception of law, the social imperative to obey it, and social culture in general.[3] Different types of lawmaking culture can be traced back to different conceptions of political power, as has been put forth by political theorist Hannah Arendt.

For the sake of this chapter, I will refer to legal culture as a set of social attitudes toward law. This may not be the most precise definition, but it will suffice. Such an understanding of a legal culture can be further divided into three subcultures: the culture of lawmaking, of law *as it is* (social attitudes toward the content of law), and of law's "aftermath" (how it is received, internalized, adjudicated, etc.). I do not claim that this division is complete (i.e., that there are no other legal subcultures), nor that those layers do not intersect. My purpose here is exclusively to show that the *process* of making law affects legal culture *indifferently* to the law's content. This is why I will concentrate exclusively on what I refer to as the culture of lawmaking.

Lawmaking is the process of creating rules which regulate life in a political society. By doing so, lawmakers pose obligations on individuals, determining what can and what cannot be done. In this sense, law is a tool of a wider political concept, that is, political power. While parliamentary lawmaking is incomparably more sophisticated than pharaoh's decision-making in ancient Egypt, what they have in common is that they regulate the lives of individuals. This is why applying theoretical considerations regarding power to the issue of lawmaking culture is attainable and, perhaps, beneficial.

---

[3] Piotr Sztompka, "From East Europeans to Europeans: Shifting collective identities and symbolic boundaries in the New Europe" (2004) 12 *European Review.*

6.2 Conceptions of power

Power is one of many notions that we use even if we are unable to fully conceptualize it. We look on those *in power*, when predicting future decisions. We obey regulations we do not like, because institutions enacting them *have power* to enforce them. We associate *power* with soldiers, police officers, and other servicemen, as they can force us to do things we do not want to. *Power* is something you must *obey*, or otherwise face consequences.

Power is not tantamount to coercion.[4] Not all decisions of those in power need to be enforced. On the contrary, the vast majority of them are voluntarily followed by society. Some of them *because* those are decisions of those in power, and some merely casually. But whenever a decision is disregarded, voluntarily or not, a reaction will inevitably be in order.

So understood, power occurs on numerous levels of social activity. Children are often tasked with various activities, and parents can think of several unpleasant consequences of their misbehavior. Referees in a game of volleyball can call out errors committed by players and award the opposite team with extra points. A judge can sentence someone for life imprisonment, had the convict committed a crime sufficiently serious. What all those cases have in common is that the person in power can determine the fate of the person who lacks that very power.[5]

Does lawmaking fit this concept of power? Do lawmakers have *power* in this sense? It is perhaps easier to associate lawmaking with political power in autocratic regimes, where people responsible for making laws are directly connected to their execution. If there was one reason that accumulated so much hatred for Tsar Nicolas II, it is probably the fact that under the Russian *samoderzhaviye* the responsibility for all of the regime's atrocities could be traced directly to the ruler. It is however not necessary for a regime to be autocratic to see the lawmaking process as a use of power. Bureaucratic legislation creates rules that are then followed by masses, even though they do not associate those rules with any particular individual. Members of party-dominated parliaments need not personally supervise adjudication of

4 Isaiah Berlin, "Two Concepts of Liberty" in *Four Essays in Liberty* (OUP 1969) 126.

5 Such understanding of power—as a characteristic that one can *have*—can be found in works, for example, of Robert Dahl ["The Concept of Power" (1957) 3 *Behavioral Science*], or Bertrand Russel (*Power: A New Social Analysis*, London 1938).

the rules they create, and rules they created are often in force long after their terms are concluded. So, while lawmakers do not possess or execute "power" in a sense a volleyball referee does, they still asymmetrically determine the lives of individuals. They do have power, only execute it indirectly. That legal norms can be understood as tools of power is only reinforced by the sentiment shared by some legal scholars, that sanctions are necessary part thereof.[6]

This understanding of power is common-sensual and matches with the literal meaning the word "power" is usually ascribed. While various concepts of power differ in numerous ways, their common ground is that they see political power as a feature *that one can have*. Power is ascribable to an individual, group, or institution. It is something that can be *shared* (think about the separation of powers), *delegated* (e.g., to local councils), *restored to someone* (after a successful counter-revolution), etc. The one who *has* power can later *exercise it* by affecting others' conduct, sometimes contrary to their will[7]. To those understanding *power* this way, it is a characteristic that one possesses.

If we accept this concept of political power, the role of law in political communities appears evident. When power is understood as the ability to bindingly command a subject, law becomes the most universal and practical tool of a ruler. While smaller, well organized communities can effectively operate with those *in power* directly commanding, or at least pass the command through their subordinates,[8] large, industrial and post-industrial societies require tools that can be abstractly applied to numerous, not individually addressed, subjects. Law *relays* the command of those in power by pointing to what is required and what is forbidden. From there, there is only one step to accepting Austin's famous idea that law itself is a command.[9]

---

6 Hans Kelsen, *Reine Rechtslehre* (Mohr Siebeck 2017) 209.

7 The question of whether exercising power occurs only when an individual changes their conduct under its influence, or even if they would act in accordance with the power wielder's will even without any imperatives is of secondary importance here.

8 One need not to resort to examples from the ancient era here. The chain of *command* in the military is so developed precisely to assure the highest possible degree of directness in passing commands. The reason for that is the need for quick adaptation, unnecessary in civilian, peacetime regulations.

9 HLA Hart, *The Concept of Law* (Joseph Raz and Penelope Bulloch eds, 2nd edn, OUP 1994) 16.

One of many authors who touched upon the issue of political power was Hannah Arendt. She saw clearly that power is usually considered a characteristic that one has. This understanding of power was traced by her to the Hebrew-Christian origins of the Western political culture. Perhaps the most apparent exercise of this type of power was God *commanding* Jews through the *Ten Commandments*. It is clear that God has the power of affecting individuals' lives, and he does so by imposing rules upon them. You can either obey and be rewarded, or you can disobey and be punished—but as long as you are a subject, the power is external. You cannot affect the rules created. Power in this sense can be divided among different *power wielders*. That is the sense of biblical *Give to Caesar what belongs to Caesar—and to God what belongs to God.*[10]

A modern, partly secularized version of this understanding of power lingers through various natural law theories. Here too, *someone* (or *something*) creates the external imperatives, which must be obeyed at all times and cannot be altered through any subjects' actions. These eternal, unalienable legal standards affect individuals, and set boundaries for the royal, and later democratic decision-making. The Hebrew-Christian concept of power is also compatible with various social contract theories. While they alter the traditional *source* of the political power (it now comes *from the* subjects), they still recognize the power wielder's competence to command individuals via law. Hobbes's example is the most apparent here, but even Locke, though he recognizes further limitations to the sovereign's power (*natural rights*), does not question *his* ability to *command* within their framework.[11]

Modern political process can hardly be construed simply as *commanding* by a depersonalized body of political representatives. It does not however imply the end of the Hebrew-Christian political tradition. On the contrary, the idea of natural rights as part of natural law, one of the defining features of modern liberalism, came around in the late eighteenth and early nineteenth century, the Age of Enlightenment. While they revolutionized liberal ideology, they evolved from earlier, Christian-dominated works in law and politics (Grotius and Aquinas are two obvious examples). The Enlightenment's revolutionary changes remained mostly within the Christian tradition.

---

[10] Matthew 22:15–21.

[11] Zbigniew Ogonowski, *Locke* (Książka i Wiedza 1979).

Indeed, the concept of natural rights does not abandon the Hebrew-Christian concept of political power but uses it. Whether rights come from God or nature, they constitute a normative order, which determines the actions of individuals. Citizens do not create rules themselves, nor can they change them (such attempts would be futile), but, as Judith Shklar put it, "pursue their own legally secured ends in accordance with a higher law"[12]. Such "legal" claims are merely actions voluntary undertaken to follow involuntarily accepted rules. When a fully secularized version of this doctrine is considered, and God removed from reasonings, natural law *becomes* the command, and thus *power*, *law*, and *command* are one and the same.

A power wielder's command may be good or bad, beneficial or harmful, utility-optimizing or utility-ineffective, but the fact remains that what is commanded is to be obeyed. Behind this lawmaking process there is a very particular culture of lawmaking. It would be one of *externality* (laws are created not by subjects, but *enacted* by an institution), *personification* (lawmaking is an activity *by* a *power wielder*, an individual or institution) and *coercion* (laws can be against one's will, and in case of disobedience, they will be enforced). Political power, through legislation, always limits the individual liberty, and thus is best avoided.[13] A protoplast of such lawmaking culture is the early Hebrew-Christian process of exercising power as recognizing and relaying God's commendations, and a prominent example would be absolute monarchy with *God's legitimacy*.

6.3 Modern conceptions of power

The Hebrew-Christian political tradition is not the only Western ideological trend to address the issue of political power. The command-obey relation is adequate in describing political situations involving monarchs, autocrats, or theocrats, but such narrative becomes less convincing when self-organizing, debating bodies are considered. While the majority of the political history of the West can be convincingly presented within the Hebrew-Christian framework, there are episodes that clearly stand out.

---

[12] Judith Shklar, "The Liberalism of Fear" in Nancy Rosenblum (ed.), *Liberalism and the Moral Life* (Harvard University Press 1989) 26.

[13] Berlin (n 4), 152.

As Arendt points out, the other tradition has roots in ancient Greek *isonomia* and Roman *res publica*. Power is not associated with the command-obey relation, but with the collectivity of action. Power is not something one can *have*, but it *occurs*, or to use Arendt's own words, "springs up" when members of society engage in a joint activity to settle their issues.[14] The decision they reach is *their own*, not external, so there is no need for it to be enforced through coercion. The ideal case, in which this understanding of power occurs, is when a community of actively engaged individuals participate in a debate to reach a common decision. The decision itself is more likely to be internalized by those who are later to implement it. While violence remains a necessary part of the Hebrew-Chrisitan concept of power, it is remarkably absent in the Greco-Roman tradition.

The question whether an exercise of power is justified is, according to Arendt, a misunderstanding. One has to see the difference between *justification*, being future-oriented, and purpose-dependent, and *legitimacy*, necessarily dependent on the past, and irrelevant of the decision's purpose. While violence almost always has *some* justification (random, pointless violence, when its doer is not even trying to present reason for it, is indeed a rare occurrence in political history), power (in the Greco-Roman tradition) does not require it at all, for the sole compromise is a reason for the decision to be accepted. Whether power really *springs up* is, however, dependent on its prior *legitimacy*, that is, the active participation and the honest belief that a given decision is taken *as a community* (Arendt says: *in concerto*). Violence, in this sense, is never legitimate. This is why, when we accept the Greco-Roman concept of power, violence and power are not compatible concepts—they are opposites.[15]

One who looks for clear examples of both understandings of power in actual history will be disappointed. Both types of power, or rather the "Greco-Roman power" and violence appear parallelly and are present in all societies to a certain degree. While we can clearly point to various regimes as more power-based (Greek poleis or the Roman republic are obvious examples), or more violence-based (we need to go back no further than twentieth century

---

14 Hannah Arendt, *On Violence* (Harcourt Brace Jovanovich 1972) 52.

15 ibid. 56.

and various totalitarian regimes),[16] elements of both social occurrences are always there. Arendt goes one step further and explains why governments resort to violence—this is the case when the government's decision is not power-supported (lacks legitimacy), so it is in need of tools that require no legitimacy, only justification—violence and commands.

It is easy to imagine power *springing up* in small, ancient city-states, where a small group of men (and I mean *men*) could spend their time at the common *agora*, having their wealth secured by their wives, subordinates, and slaves. The impracticality of such political setting in ever growing states, both territoriality and administratively, led to an eventual fall of the Roman republic, and a period of more than one and a half millennium of violence-dominated politics, with few noble examples such as the Venice Republic, or the Nobleman Republic in Poland.[17] The modern English, American, and French revolutions were all directed against the abuse of violence, a rule that lacked legitimacy. With heads of tyrants properly cut off and "power" vacuums apparent, the revolutionaries needed to imbed their trust in something else.

The birth of representative government marks a symbolic return of the Greco-Roman political tradition to Western political thought.[18] While the citizens (now also women) usually do not make the legal decisions directly, they get to influence the composition of the government, sometimes by electing representatives, and always by the ability to express their views and beliefs. Such a government may claim to have legitimacy, but in order for it to be truly so, its citizens need not only to be procedurally allowed to elect or express themselves—they also have to *meaningfully do so*. The constitution of the USSR had a long catalog of subjective rights, and elections took place at several levels, from local, to central, and yet one can hardly claim that the decision-making process in the Soviet Union was "republican" in any reasonable way. Yet we need not to resort to totalitarian examples to show the importance of engagement when it comes to legitimacy. Modern, large-scale democracies, where citizens limit their political activities to casting

---

16 This was the main topic of Arendt's best-known works on totalitarianism, see: Hannah Arendt, *Eichmann in Jerusalem: A Report on the Banality of Evil* (Viking Press 1963).

17 Andrzej Dziadzio, *Polski model "rządów prawa" a europejska wizja "państwa prawa" z XIX wieku* (Wolters Kluwer 2012).

18 Arendt (n 14) 41.

ballots every couple of years, with little understanding of politics, and even less will to change it, have little more to do with Greco-Roman power than authoritarian regimes altogether.

Post-WW2 constitutionalism has widely adopted the vision of lawmaking by the parliament elected in popular vote. By doing so, it seems, the Greco-Roman notion of power was accepted as one better suited for modern societies. While there are obvious problems with actual participation in the decision-making process, often referred to as the "democracy deficit," at least the institutional setting seems to allow the government to seek legitimacy, and rule through power, instead of violence.[19] To use Arendt's words, "it is the people's support that lends power to the institutions of a country, and this support is but the continuation of the consent that brought the laws into existence to begin with."[20]

This modern variation of the Greco-Roman concept of power, with its institutional and political framework, establishes the foundation for a different culture of lawmaking, than the Hebrew-Christian tradition did. Laws are created by the government and parliament with majoritarian support. They have the responsibility to represent, and—when required—to consult the public on their decisions, and for doing so they answer when the next electoral cycle begins. The laws they create may not suit everyone, and sometimes may not be most fortunate, but they are based upon a prior legitimacy ("they may be bad laws, but they are *our* laws"). The culture of lawmaking in Greco-Roman tradition is one of *internality* (internal origin of rules), *collectivity* (social process of making rules) and *internalization* (a general lack of need for violent enforcement).

6.4 Human rights and power

Much of what constitutes the modern political institutions was created as a remedy for violent, command-based government. This is where liberal right-based ideologies meet with republican non-domination doctrines.[21] Republicanism,

---

19 This is particularly relevant in the debate on legitimacy of EU institutions, as an argument often raised against them highlights the lack or the insufficiency of the popular participation in the decision-making process, or the so-called "democracy deficit." See: Pippa Norris, "Representation and the democratic deficit" (1997) 32 *European Journal of Political Research* 273.

20 Arendt (n 14) 41.

21 Phillip Pettit, "Three Mistakes about Democracy" (2015) 2 *Kilikya Felsefe Dergisi* 4.

in Arendt's sense, does not equal democracy—its requirements are higher, for the actual participation of citizens, not merely via the election, but also in everyday political life, is necessary for the *power* to spring up.[22] Proponents of the Greco-Roman understanding of power tend to believe that such participation provides the best guarantee of a government that respects, supports, and allows citizens to pursue their goals. Institutional setting is there to facilitate, but not to replace the process of making decisions (laws), a process that itself is as important as the result. This belief seems to underlie much of the republican spirit of the first half of the twentieth century.[23]

The tragedy of the Second World War profoundly affected political theory. The fact that the Nazis originally came to *power* through a democratic procedure was highlighted by various liberal thinkers, who argued for more institutional control of the political process. This led to a post-war rebirth of the natural rights doctrine. The liberals, who had previously supported the lawmaking process by a representative parliament, as long as it did not infiltrate the individual personal sphere, have now highlighted the importance of some standards being respected at all times and at all levels of governance, indifferent of what the positive law may say.[24]

This fundamental change in beliefs is clearly observable in jurisprudence. It is hard for a better example than one of Gustav Radbruch. Being Germany's most prominent legal philosopher, his pre-war philosophy, even though heavily influenced by neo-Kantianism, led to a fundamentally positivistic conclusion: that a valid rule of law, however unjust it may seem, must be adjudicated by the judge according to lawmaker's will.[25] If such a positivistic conclusion is collocated with a republican lawmaking process, we are close to reaching the discursive character of legal norms, a key feature of the lawmaking culture in the Greco-Roman political tradition. However, Radbruch

---

22 Hannah Arendt, *On Revolution* (Viking Books 1963) 30.

23 It would be fair to say that political thinkers who shared this sentiment were in minority at that time, when various authoritarian authors, right as Schmitt and left as Lenin, were active, but many Western states still had institutions meant for political deliberation.

24 H. L. A. Hart "Between Utility and Rights" in *Essays in Jurisprudence and Philosophy* (OUP 1983) 202.

25 H. L. A. Hart, "Positivism and the Separation of Law and Morals" in *Essays in Jurisprudence and Philosophy* (OUP 1983) 72.

reviewed his beliefs during the war. Later, in a short lecture "Five Minutes for Legal Philosophy" (1945), he claimed that "only a dogmatic skeptic may still entertain doubts" about human rights existence.[26] This later led to him formulating his famous Formula, according to which a judge has an obligation *not* to adjudicate a legal norm that was created in the lawmaking process, when it violates those ultimate pre-political principles, human rights.[27] This post-war rebirth of a non-positivist viewpoint later contributed to creation of some most fundamental works in modern liberal thought, Rawls's, Nozick's, and Dworkin's among them.[28]

The almost universal recognition of the very existence of human rights[29] creates particular challenges for the lawmaking culture. In the traditional republican concept of power, the source of decisions (that translate to legal norms via legislation) is located in the debating parliament, which has a democratic, indirect legitimacy. When the notion of pre-political standards (human rights) is adopted, this legitimacy is insufficient for a decision (legal norm) to be considered valid, for it requires additional congruence with this standard. If the task of ensuring such a congruence was entrusted to the very same individuals responsible for creating rules, any effective control would be virtual. The task thus needed to be handed to someone else, preferably to someone impartial and professional, and so it happened that there was an apparently perfect social group to handle it—judges.

The idea of judicial control of the legislative process is not new. While its roots date back to pre-Enlightenment times,[30] two main models were developed in the nineteenth century. The American, dispersed control ("judicial review") came into being after the Madison v. Marbury case, while the continental model of centralized, Tribunal control was introduced in Austrian

---

[26] Gustav Radbruch, "Fünf Minuten Rechtsphilosophie," *Rhein-Neckar-Zeitung*, September 12, 1945.

[27] Robert Alexy, "Gustav Radbruchs Rechtsbegriff" in Martin Borowski (ed.), *Modern German Non-Positivism*, (Mohr Siebeck 2019) 17.

[28] H. L. A. Hart, "Utilitarianism and Natural Rights," in *Essays in Jurisprudence and Philosophy* (OUP 1983) 183.

[29] Joseph Raz, *Human Rights Without Foundations*, Oxford Legal Studies Research Paper 14/2007, <https://papers.ssrn.com/sol3/papers.cfm?abstract_id=999874> accessed August 26, 2024.

[30] Andrzej Dziadzio, *Powszechna historia prawa* (Wydawnictwo Naukowe PWN 2008) 135.

Empire, and further developed by Hans Kelsen.[31] The latter is particularly important in the Central and Eastern European context, as the Austrian Tribunal was a model for the German Federal Constitutional Court, and this so-called Karlsruhe model was later adopted in post-soviet European republics, such as Poland or Hungary.

The question of what the competences of a Constitutional Court judge are, is far from trivial. As Piotr Tuleja points out, there are at least two models of them.[32] The first is the "civil-servant model," where a judge is just an official, who performs his duties according to existing law. In this case, the Constitutional Court's tasks are limited to examining the congruence of the challenged laws with the Constitution and invalidating the norm if (and only if) an *incongruence* appears. This is what Kelsen saw as the role of the Court in the first place. However, in the second, or "imperious" model, inspired predominantly by Anglo-Saxon jurisprudence, the constitutional judges shall not only examine the literal text of the law, but creatively interpret it to reach a conclusion best serving the fundamental task of human rights protection.

The post-war renaissance of human rights led to a shift from "civil-servant" to "imperious" model in many continental judiciary systems.[33] Judges of many constitutional courts are now not only bound to check the law's congruence with the Constitution, but also to determine the level of individual rights protection, and sometimes to directly point to institutional solutions that best solve such issues. This is most apparent in cases when the proposed law is neither *congruent* nor *incongruent* with a presented constitutional sample (it is, as the Polish public law doctrine calls it, *not incongruent*).[34] A civil-servant

---

[31] Andrzej Dziadzio, "Między ideą a praktyką ustrojową: o drodze Austrii do sądu konstytucyjnego" (2018) *Forum prawnicze*.

[32] Piotr Tuleja, "Czy Konstytucja jest potrzebna do wymierzania sprawiedliwości?" (2019) 2 *Iustitia* 82.

[33] Those are naturally ideal models. They never appear in real institutional settings to a full degree, nor do they appear exclusively. However, most institutional settings can be put on a scale between those two benchmarks.

[34] This is a very specific case in which there is no necessary relation (of congruence or incongruence) between the questioned regulation and the constitutional provision. Rulings of this type may appear in two cases—when the constitutional control motion was formulated improperly (say, someone questioned the law on elections as violating right to property), or—more importantly—when the constitutional norm is insufficiently specific to clearly outline its relation to questioned regulation.

judge will simply see no reason for such a norm to be addressed by a Constitutional Court at all. An imperious judge, however, may see this as a chance to propose a solution that will best fit the requirements posed by human rights. This last type of activity can well be called *judicial lawmaking*.[35]

6.5 Power under the imperious model

The shift from the civil servant to the imperious model has profound consequences for our debate about power. While both may appear to have transferred some of the competences from representative, legitimate bodies, to expert, non-majoritarian organs, the difference between them is of fundamental importance.

A Constitutional Court in the civil-servant model adjudicates exclusively in relation to the Constitution[36]. The Constitution is adopted *by a representative body*, to be the general act, and this very body *had legitimacy*. Constitutional adjudication is merely ensuring that officials respect various levels of importance of norms, all of which were created in a republican process. The fact that Constitutions were adopted in a legitimate way is further reinforced by the fact that they can be *changed*, when enough popular support is amassed. In such a case, the power would spring up again at this fundamental level. Judges do not create any norms, but only ensure that what was previously accepted, is in fact respected.

A Constitutional Court in the imperious model has competence to refer to standards that the Constitution may recognize, but which reach far beyond its text. By doing so, it challenges the will of a representative body, based not only on what was legitimately accepted by this body, but also on certain standards that are somehow prior and superior to this legitimacy. When judges create norms, they do not refer to existing, legitimate standards, but also to standards that may have never been legitimately agreed upon by a republican body.

Choosing between the two models of a Constitutional Court is in fact a choice between two combinations of decisions and normative sources. In the

---

35 Tuleja (n 32) 84.

36 And international law. This is an obvious simplification for the sake of keeping those ideal models clear. What matters is an inclination to either *limit* normative sources of decisions (*civil-servant model*) or to *extend* it (*imperious model*).

civil-servant model, *all* norms come from bodies legitimated in a republican manner; in an imperious model, *some* norms come from such bodies, while others are *external* to them. It is a judge who is responsible for deciding whether those external standards are applicable in particular cases, and if so, what their consequences are for other regulations. This is why Dworkin refers to judges as "princes of law."[37]

But the choice between those two models is much more than merely a selection of the quantity of normative sources—it is precisely a choice between the recognized types of power. While lawmaking by a representative parliament fits the Greco-Roman tradition of power as a collectively *sprung* occurrence, the judicial lawmaking does not even attempt to do so. An active judge is to recognize an external, eternal and overriding standard, and to apply it even against the popular will. That a decision may go against the majoritarian will is considered by many liberals as a standalone virtue. When he does so, his decision becomes a rule that is enforceable. This decision becomes part of the body of the law of land, even though this process has never been, directly or not, legitimized by a political community in the Greco-Roman sense. Power has never *sprung up*. What is left is a command by a judge and the obligation to obey by the public.

Again, this has absolutely nothing to do with the content of the decision itself. The judge may offer an extremely persuasive argument in favor of such a lawmaking ruling, usually based upon a reference to human rights.[38] But again, if we follow Arendt's reasoning, what they offer is merely a *justification*. A lawmaking decision by a non-representative, non-republican body, based upon standards external to prior republican agreements, may be well justified, but will never have *legitimacy*. This is why in the Greco-Roman tradition, judicial lawmaking is an example not of *power*, but of *violence*.

Constitutional Court's judges are usually elderly men, and the process of their decision-making obviously does not resemble the violence-based *modus operandi* of typical authoritarian regimes. But whatever is decided by them becomes the law, and this law may be enforced also with use of actual force. Modern history knows numerous cases of protest sprung by controversial

---

[37] Marek Zirk-Sadowski, "Wprowadzenie" in Ronald Dworkin, *Imperium prawa* (Wolters Kluwer Polska 2006) XXIII.

[38] Tuleja (n 32) 84.

rulings, and it is not seldom for them to evolve into open clashes.[39] Such a lawmaking process has little to do with republican vision of power.

6.6 Polish conceptions of power

Poland is among few European states that happens to have a rich and century-old republican tradition. Among many principles of the *Nobleman Republic* (*Rzeczpospolita Szlachecka*) were the concept of popular agreement on new laws, and the primacy of law over monarch's will. Andrzej Dziadzio goes as far as to claim that 1st Polish Republic (i.e., approx. 1500s–1795) may have been a protoplast of a *Rechtsstaat*,[40] and while the often-mentioned proverb *Lex est Rex in Polonia* had little to do with our understanding of the rule of law, it highlighted the basic rejection of arbitrariness and domination in relations of power.[41] While a holistic analysis of the 1st Republic tends to be negative,[42] one cannot question the fact that some institutional solutions were way ahead of their time.

The interwar period in Polish history was predominantly a time of rebuilding statehood, marked by desperate attempts to bring cohesion to a state made up of five (Austrian, Hungarian, Russian, Congress Poland, and German) different legal, monetary, and institutional systems. While two constitutions came to existence in that period (a democratic one in 1923 and an authoritarian one in 1935), their value, in the modern-constitutionalism sense, was rather limited. They predominantly consisted of procedural provisions and institutional settings, offering little to no insight of political principles underlying the community. But even those two constitutions, in particular the latter, authoritarian one, had strong republican symbolics to it. The Constitution of 1935 begins with 10 articles commonly referred to as a *Pole's Decalogue*, which highlighted moral and political responsibilities

---

39 Arendt (n 14) 29.

40 Dziadzio (n 17).

41 Wacław Uruszczak, *Historia państwa i prawa polskiego. Tom I*, (Wolters Kluwer 2010), 142.

42 Due to particularism of the richest layer of nobility, and the ability to influence politics through the lower layer by outside powers—bear in mind that noblemen were, in theory, equal—state ultimately failed to protect itself against Austrians, Prussians and Russians, what led to an over a century long period of Partitions.

toward the motherland. But again, as Tuleja points out, to look for an inspiration for a modern constitution in those texts is a task deemed to failure.[43] Constitutionalism in the communism period in Poland has its own distinctive republican sense (as far as one understands the *republic* as a community of working people), but its influence on modern politics is neglectable.

All those facts led Lech Morawski to a rather evident conclusion, that Polish constitutional tradition is predominantly republican.[44] It would therefore imply that the culture of lawmaking in Poland is more likely to be one of the Greco-Roman, parliamentary tradition. Parliamentarism is a well-developed notion in Polish political thought, and while both modern, and historical assemblages were often extremely emotional, vindictive, and seldom conclusive, they remained the key factor in the lawmaking process. Judiciary independence has been recognized since times of the 1st Republic (impartiality was considered a guarantee of protection of individual freedoms),[45] but it only referred to adjudication, never to lawmaking.[46]

The post-communist transformation after 1989 was the first time in more than 200 years when Poles had the opportunity to create their constitutional and institutional system truly by *themselves*. The decision makers of that time were well aware that there was a specific *window of opportunity*, when society could be motivated enough to participate in a wide constitutional debate—after all, the Solidarity movement attracted, at its height, more than ten million members. It quickly turned out that the Solidarity dominated, but highly diverse parliament (there were no electoral thresholds at that time), was unable to pursue any reasonable constitutional agenda, and the debate

---

43 Tuleja (n 32), 81.

44 Lech Morawski's presentation at the Visegrad Constitutional Court Head Judges Meeting in Budapest, 15–February 17, 2017, *Spór o tożsamość konstytucyjną Polaków*, <https://trybunal.gov.pl/wiadomosci/uroczystosci-spotkania-wyklady/art/9566-budapeszt-spotkanie-prezesow-sadow-konstytucyjnych-panstw-grupy-wyszehradzkiej> accessed August 26, 2024.

45 Uruszczak (n 41) 194.

46 It would be wrong to say that Polish legal culture, especially in times of the 1st Republic, is of positivistic sentiment. Noblemen associated adjudication with justice more than they did with the rule of law. The concept of precedent rulings was, however, never accepted, perhaps *because of* the strong belief that participation in the lawmaking process is what makes it legitimate.

seemed to go nowhere. Time went by, and Poles were not a step closer to a new constitution.

In those circumstances, another center of power began to pursue a more ambitious agenda. The Constitutional Tribunal was established back in the late communist era, and at that time consisted of some of the most influential Polish public law scholars. It is them who took upon themselves the task of setting fundamental constitutional principles, what happened in a series of milestone rulings, in Polish doctrine referred to as the "*lawmaking* period of the Constitutional Tribunal." Their evaluation of basic values and principles is what later became a core of the Polish Constitution of 1997. What they agreed upon has a fundamentally liberal characteristics, where republican elements are effectively absent.[47]

My point is not to argue whether this particular set of values was proper or not. My mere purpose is to show that the very idea that judges can validly set core principles underlying the political system takes its legitimacy from a different, Hebrew-Christian tradition. Such arguments may well be found in the political writings of Locke, but what influenced judges of the Constitutional Tribunal incomparably more is the neo-Kantianism underlying post-war German constitutionalism. Indeed, *Grundgesetz* operates on a different philosophical assumption than any republican setting, with human dignity and basic rights being *pre-political* (pre-state), a concept completely absents in Arendt's Greco-Roman concept of power. The reasoning of the Constitutional Tribunal often resembles the well-known *recognition* of existing, natural standards, or to use other words, what the natural law *commands*. The philosophy of power behind the lawmaking activity of the Constitutional Tribunal is one of Hebrew-Christian tradition.

Morawski is right to recognize that judicial activism is an alien element in Polish constitutional tradition. He is also probably right, when he ascribes the shift to liberal philosophy. In any case, by setting the fundamental principles of the 1997 Constitution on their own, the respectable judges of the Constitutional Tribunal broke up with a long republican tradition of Polish constitutionalism, and installed a new, liberal and neo-Kantian instead. Even constitutional law scholars recognize that modern Polish constitution is

---

[47] Wojciech Ciszewski, "Republikańskie odczytanie Konstytucji Rzeczypospolitej Polskiej" (2017) 4 *Przegląd Konstytucyjny*.

predominantly an adopted one.[48] Similar thing, to my knowledge, happened in Hungary.[49] So, in this sense, the Polish judiciary is Janus-faced—it wears the mask of republican restraint in law and in tradition, but shows the liberal face in practice and aspirations.

Among many questions this transformation poses, one is related to the culture of lawmaking—can such a voluntary action of a group of 15 people change the way people think about such a fundamental phenomenon as making political decisions? There are good reasons to believe that the set of principles behind the liberal Constitution were never internalized by the majority of Poles. Only two days after the Constitution went into effect, two conservative MPs forcibly installed a Christian cross in the parliament building. They did it at night, with no approval of any institution, broke some furniture in the process, and yet no one seriously considered removing the cross to this day, even though the principle of secularity is explicitly secured in the Constitution.

But an example even more apparent is still fresh in the memory of many Poles. In 2020, the Constitutional Tribunal ruled that abortion in case of lethal fetal abnormalities was unconstitutional, what sprung a series of mass protests called *Black protests* (after the color worn by the protesters), which ended up being the most numerous protests against Law and Justice regime in Poland[50] and seriously contributed to the regime's overthrow in the parliamentary election of 2023. What is symbolic is that protesters seldom participated in an actual debate whether the ruling was constitutionally valid or not (some authors argued that it is essentially coherent with earlier rulings of the CT),[51] but highlighted that it is *not a judge's decision to make.* Protests were sometimes met with a significant dose of police brutality.[52]

---

48 Tuleja (n 32) 84.

49 László Sólyom, "Aufbau und dogmatische Fundierung der ungarischen Verfasssungsgerichtsbarkeit" (2000) 3–4 *Osteuropa Recht.*

50 Elżbieta Korolczuk, Beata Kowalska, Jennifer Ramme, and Claudia Snochowska-Gonzalez (eds), *Bunt kobiet. Czarne Protesty i Strajki Kobiet*, Europejskie Centrum Solidarności, <https://old2022.ecs.gda.pl/library/File/nauka/e-booki/raport/ECS_raport_buntkobiet.pdf> accessed August 26, 2024

51 Rafał Adamus, "Przesłanka eugeniczna (embriopatologiczna) jako przesłanka legalnego przerywania ciąży. Glosa do wyroku TK z dnia 22 października 2020 r., K 1/20" (2020) 11 *Palestra.*

52 "Strajk Kobiet: Policja jest brutalna i łamie prawo, bo pozwala na to Kaczyński" (2020) *Dziennik Gazeta Prawna*, December 2, 2020.

This highlights a key difference between both traditions of power—what is *power* in a Hebrew-Christian, judicial activism sense, that is, a command originating from the natural law, that needs to be enforced, is merely *violence* in a Greco-Roman, republican sense, violence directed against individuals, who gathered to take matters into their own hands. Perhaps those protests are where the *power* may have actually sprung up. Given that not even 9 percent of Poles support the ruling,[53] and the results of 2023 parliamentary elections, one can imagine that support for command-based politics is lower than many have anticipated.

6.7 Conclusion

My point in this essay was not to argue for any of the two distinctive cultures of lawmaking, nor to advocate for the superiority of the Greco-Roman concept of power. Each of them has a unique set of advantages and disadvantages, and it is my belief that making an *in abstracto* decision on one's superiority is futile. Constitutional order may or may not have its foundations in political culture—in the latter case however, its efficiency in serving the community is significantly reduced.

Republican tradition has much to offer, and to many it may represent the very ideal the democratic states of the twenty-first century should aspire to. It is, however, essential to understand, that accepting republican tradition significantly limits the possibility of implementing solutions of Hebrew-Christian origin, relying on a command-obey relation—such solutions will seldom be legitimized in a republican sense, and unless they casually correlate to a current political consensus, they will need to be enforced through violence.

It is perhaps very telling that two states considered Pariahs of liberal Europe, Poland, and Hungary, are the two, in which constitutional orders were created predominantly through an implementation of foreign solutions and judicial activism. If this relation is anything more than a causal correlation, it only reinforces the belief that some steps in creating a political

53 "Dwa lata po wyroku TK ws. aborcji. Pozytywnie decyzję ocenia 8,9 proc. Polaków" (2022) *Rzeczpospolita*, October 21, 2022, <https://www.rp.pl/spoleczenstwo/art37276691-dwa-lata-po-wyroku-tk-ws-aborcji-pozytywnie-decyzje-ocenia-8-9-proc-polakow> accessed August 26, 2024.

community cannot be skipped, and the process of accepting common basic regulation may be inevitably lengthy and painful. For shortcuts will show. And they will show painfully.

Bibliography

——— "Dwa lata po wyroku TK ws. aborcji. Pozytywnie decyzję ocenia 8,9 proc. Polaków" (2022) *Rzeczpospolita*, October 21, 2022, <https://www.rp.pl/spoleczenstwo/art37276691-dwa-lata-po-wyroku-tk-ws-aborcji-pozytywnie-decyzje-ocenia-8-9-proc-polakow> accessed August 26, 2024.

——— "Strajk Kobiet: Policja jest brutalna i łamie prawo, bo pozwala na to Kaczyński" (2020) *Dziennik Gazeta Prawna*, December 2, 2020 Adamus R, "Przesłanka eugeniczna (embriopatologiczna) jako przesłanka legalnego przerywania ciąży. Glosa do wyroku TK z dnia 22 października 2020 r., K 1/20" (2020) 11 *Palestra*.

Alexy R., "Gustav Radbruchs Rechtsbegriff" in M. Borowski (ed.), *Modern German Non-Positivism*, (Mohr Siebeck 2019).

Arendt H., *On Violence* (Harcourt Brace Jovanovich 1972).

——— *On Revolution* (Viking Books 1963).

——— *Eichmann in Jerusalem: A Report on the Banality of Evil* (Viking Press 1963).

Berlin I., "Two Concepts of Liberty" in *Four Essays in Liberty* (OUP 1969).

Ciszewski W., "Republikańskie odczytanie Konstytucji Rzeczypospolitej Polskiej" (2017) 4 *Przegląd Konstytucyjny*.

Dahl R., "The Concept of Power" (1957) 3 *Behavioral Science*.

Dziadzio A., *Polski model "rządów prawa" a europejska wizja "państwa prawa" z XIX wieku* (Wolters Kluwer 2012).

Dziadzio A., "Między ideą a praktyką ustrojową: o drodze Austrii do sądu konstytucyjnego" (2018) *Forum prawnicze*.

Dziadzio A., *Powszechna historia prawa* (Wydawnictwo Naukowe PWN 2008).

Ekiert G., "Prawidłowości transformacji w Europie Wschodniej' (2011) 1 *Studia Socjologiczne*.

H. L. A. Hart, *The Concept of Law* (Joseph Raz and Penelope Bulloch eds, 2nd edn, OUP 1994).

——— "Between Utility and Rights" in *Essays in Jurisprudence and Philosophy* (OUP 1983).

——— "Positivism and the Separation of Law and Morals" in *Essays in Jurisprudence and Philosophy* (OUP 1983).

Kelsen H., *Reine Rechtslehre* (Mohr Siebeck 2017).

Morawski L.'s presentation at the Visegrad Constitutional Court Head Judges Meeting in Budapest, February 15–17, 2017, *Spór o tożsamość konstytucyjną Polaków*, <https://trybunal.gov.pl/wiadomosci/uroczystosci-spotkania-wyklady/art/9566-budapeszt-spotkanie-prezesow-sadow-konstytucyjnych-panstw-grupy-wyszehradzkiej> accessed August 26, 2024.

Norris P., "Representation and the democratic deficit" (1997) 32 *European Journal of Political Research* 273.

Ogonowski Z., *Locke* (Książka i Wiedza 1979).

Pettit P., "Three Mistakes about Democracy" (2015) 2 *Kilikya Felsefe Dergisi* 4.

Radbruch G., "Fünf Minuten Rechtsphilosophie," *Rhein-Neckar-Zeitung*, September 12, 1945.

Russel B., *Power: A New Social Analysis*, London 1938.

Raz J., *Human Rights Without Foundations*, Oxford Legal Studies Research Paper 14/2007, <https://papers.ssrn.com/sol3/papers.cfm?abstract_id=999874> accessed August 26, 2024.

Shklar J., "The Liberalism of Fear" in N. Rosenblum (ed.), *Liberalism and the Moral Life* (Harvard University Press 1989).

Sólyom L., "Aufbau und dogmatische Fundierung der ungarischen Verfasssungsgerichtsbarkeit" (2000) 3–4 *Osteuropa Recht.*

Sztompka P., "From East Europeans to Europeans: Shifting collective identities and symbolic boundaries in the New Europe" (2004) 12 *European Review.*

Tuleja P., "Czy Konstytucja jest potrzebna do wymierzania sprawiedliwości?" (2019) 2 *Iustitia* 82.

Uruszczak W., *Historia państwa i prawa polskiego. Tom I*, (Wolters Kluwer 2010).

Zirk-Sadowski M., “Wprowadzenie” in Ronald Dworkin, *Imperium prawa* (Wolters Kluwer Polska 2006).

Korolczuk E., Kowalska B., Ramme J. and Snochowska-Gonzalez C. (eds), *Bunt kobiet. Czarne Protesty i Strajki Kobiet*, Europejskie Centrum Solidarności, <https://old2022.ecs.gda.pl/library/File/nauka/e-booki/raport/ECS_raport_buntkobiet.pdf> accessed August 26, 2024.

Index

Central and Eastern European Forum for Legal, Political, and Social Theory Yearbook

Edited by Jürgen Busch / Péter Cserne / Michael Hein / Miklós Könczöl / Miodrag Jovanović / Marta Soniewicka

Vol. 1 Péter Cserne / Miklós Könczöl (eds.): Legal and Political Theory in the Post-National Age. Selected papers presented at the Second Central and Eastern European Forum for Legal, Political and Social Theorists (Budapest, 21–22 May 2010). 2011.

Vol. 2 Miodrag A. Jovanović / Bojan Spaić (eds.): Jurisprudence and Political Philosophy in the 21st Century. Reassessing Legacies. 2012.

Vol. 3 Péter Cserne / Miklós Könczöl / Marta Soniewicka (eds.): The Rule of Law and the Challenges to Jurisprudence. Selected papers presented at the Fourth Central and Eastern European Forum for Legal, Political and Social Theorists, Celje, 23–24 March 2012. 2014.

Vol. 4 Antonia Geisler / Michael Hein / Siri Hummel (eds.): Law, Politics, and the Constitution. New Perspectives from Legal and Political Theory. 2014.

Vol. 5 Luka Burazin / Đorđe Gardašević / Alessio Sardo (eds.): Law and State. Classical Paradigms and Novel Proposals. 2015.

Vol. 6 Martin Belov (ed.): Global Governance and Its Effects on State and Law. 2016.

Vol. 7 Fekete, Balázs / Gárdos- Orosz, Fruzsina (eds.): Central and Eastern European Socio-Political and Legal Transition Revisited. 2018.

Vol. 8 Alexandra Mercescu (ed.): Constitutional Identities in Central and Eastern Europe. 2020.

Vol. 9 Tomáš Gábriš / Ján Sombati (eds.): Central and Eastern Europe as a Double Periphery? Volume of proceedings from the 11th CEE Forum Conference in Bratislava. 2020.

Vol. 10 Stefan Mayr / Andreas Orator (eds.): Populism, Popular Sovereignty, and Public Reason. 2021.

Vol. 11 Michał Paździora / Michał Stambulski (eds.): Democracy, Legal Education and the Political. 2023.

Vol. 12 Petr Agha / Jan Géryk (eds.): Political Imagination and Utopian Energies in Central and Eastern Europe. 2024.

Vol. 13 Áron Fábián / Márton Matyasovszky-Németh (eds.): Legal Culture and Identity in Central and Eastern Europe. 2026.

www.peterlang.com

www.ingramcontent.com/pod-product-compliance
Ingram Content Group UK Ltd.
Pitfield, Milton Keynes, MK11 3LW, UK
UKHW041827031026
15587UKWH00002B/618

9 783631 908556